THE
HIGH-VALUE
MANAGER

DEVELOPING THE CORE COMPETENCIES YOUR ORGANIZATION DEMANDS

Florence M. Stone & Randi T. Sachs

American Management Association

New York • Atlanta • Boston • Chicago • Kansas City • San Francisco • Washington, D.C.
Brussels • Mexico City • Tokyo • Toronto

Library of Congress Cataloging-in-Publication Data

Stone, Florence M.
    The high-value manager : developing the core competencies your
organization demands / Florence M. Stone and Randi T. Sachs.
        p. cm.
    Includes index.
    ISBN 0-8144-0298-4
    1. Executive ability.   2. Total quality management.   I. Sachs,
Randi Toler.   II. Title.
    HD38.2.S765   1995
    658.4'092—dc20   95-37972
                                                                   CIP

Printing number

10 9 8 7 6 5

Contents

Introduction

If you have survived the reengineering at your company, don't assume that you need not worry until the next downturn. Reengineering/downsizing, whether a viable strategy or not, has become a strategy and may be repeated in good times as well as bad; economic stability doesn't reduce the likelihood of further reorganization, even downsizing. The possibility of your losing your job is heightened by the ever increasing changes likely occurring within your organization.

We can expect the trend toward leaner managerial organizations to continue into the future. Managerial holes in organization charts will be plugged by nonstaff (consulting) managers. Firms have discovered that they can fill not only low-level positions with contract employees.

At the same time companies downsize or rightsize, they are restructuring or reorganizing—in many instances, to team-based work processes that will make you and other managers and supervisors into team developers and coaches. You will need the skills and abilities these leaner, restructured organizations demand.

Professional obsolescence is a possibility. Responsibilities that once were important are no longer so. Others that weren't so important have become critical. As responsibilities have shifted, so have the skills, abilities, knowledge, and attitudes that make for *high-value* managers.

The words "high value" are emphasized for reason. Today's leaner, restructured organizations can't tolerate mediocrity. The fewer the managers, the more critical their performance in achieving strategic intent—and the higher the stakes in managerial recruitment and evaluation. With fewer managers on staff, companies are looking for ways to maximize the contribution of their human assets.

What are the managerial skills, abilities, and attitudes most important to most companies today?

The issue has become so vital that it is making some human resources consulting firms wealthy. Companies are contracting to have these consultants interview senior and middle managers and team leaders to determine what makes high-value managerial performance, then are using this information to make recruitment, training, performance evaluation, promotion, and, yes, even layoff decisions. These organizations believe the presence of these competencies can radically improve their competitive position, just as can a new distribution network or a new product line. These companies expect that competency modeling, which is what the process is called, will give them data that will enable them to receive a better return on managerial salaries—in the form of higher productivity and greater results.

Some competencies are unique to organizations' strategic direction or industry. Others are shared in common with most other companies operating in today's fast-changing times. It is the latter that are described here.

This book does not purport to be based on the kind of competency modeling that high-priced consulting firms offer. Rather, it is based on the results of research involving the readers of a number of periodicals published by the American Management Association and interviews with trainers and senior managers over the last three years. Its purpose is to make today's managers and team leaders or coaches aware of those skills, abilities, and attitudes most valued today. But knowing what those valued assets are will not in itself enable you to advance in your organization, let alone survive the next managerial cuts. So we are including a self-inventory that should help you evaluate yourself in these new critical skills, abilities, and attitudes.

The self-test in the first chapter asks you to answer honestly how you would behave in a particular situation. While you may know how you *should* behave, it is important for your career that you react to the question as quickly as you might react to the real-life situation. Once you have completed the questionnaire, you can evaluate your responses as explained in the second chapter in the section. We've included references to allow you to build skills in any areas in which you identify deficiencies.

This is a wonderful opportunity to determine your managerial capability in the boundaryless management age that is growing on us. But should you have some doubts about your findings after completing the test, Chapter 2 also offers a second tool you can use to measure your managerial capability. At the end of the chapter is a series of questions you can ask those individuals with whom you interact most frequently: your own manager, your employees, your peers, and your customers. Intuitively, you probably know where your strengths lie, and you may want to ask as well that person you see each morning in the mirror how well you are adapting to the new competencies demanded of you.

Some HR consulting firms provide companies with these broad pictures of their managerial talent. We think you can benefit by gaining insights right now into how people view your performance. Not only may the results of your queries be enlightening, but asking those with whom you work for their input tells them that you respect their judgment and value having a good working relationship with them.

Asking these questions may enlighten you about the cause of problems between you and your boss that you were not aware of before, thereby smoothing your work relationship with him or her. Your peers will see a request from you as evidence that you want to be cooperative and that you respect their judgment. Both are important to spanning boundaries, a critical advantage in today's unboxed organizations. Your employees will respect you if you let it be known that you welcome their criticisms. And your customers, internal or external, will find that you truly do believe in providing high-value customer service if you ask them how well you are providing for their needs.

Section I

Succeeding in Today's Leaner Organizations

Organizations are demanding very different managerial skills today than they did a few years ago. Their need for these skills is so critical that they are spending tens of thousands of dollars to have companies identify those managers within their organizations with these critical skills. The results of these studies are being used to determine whom to promote as well as whom to hire and whom to lay off.

We surveyed both middle management and senior management ranks to identify those competencies that most organizations regard as essential to their competitive survival. And here we offer eighty competencies that our studies show you will need to succeed in today's organizations. We've organized this book to enable you to measure your competencies—to determine your managerial fitness for today's leaner organizations—and to develop fully the skills, abilities, and attitudes you need now and into the future, as functional silos continue to fall, teams become the means by which more work is done, and positional authority increasingly becomes less important.

The first chapter in this section will enable you to test your response to fifty situations. Then, in Chapter 2, you can examine, privately, your responses, in light of the competencies our studies identified. Chapter 2 also includes a list of questions to enable you to confirm how you measure up to the needs of today's restructured organizations.

1

Are You a High-Value Manager? A Self-Inventory Test

To determine those skills most critical to their organizations, companies engage in behavior event interviewing in which both supermanagers and average managers are interviewed to determine those skills, behaviors, traits, or attitudes that differentiate one from the other. The test below is designed to do somewhat the same: to help determine those managers most skilled to address situations likely to arise in today's less structured, leaner organizations—to separate high-value managers from less coveted ones.

In completing the test below, it is critical that you be as honest with yourself as possible. We cannot overemphasize that.

Each statement has three possible answers. Circle the action you would most likely take or statement with which you would most agree. (In some instances there may be two actions that are acceptable, but one is preferable.) Upon completion, you can check your answers in Chapter 2. That's where you will also find references to the specific competencies. Then you need only go to the competency index at the end of the book to determine the nature of the competency and chapter in which you can read more about that particular competency.

As you do the test, don't think through your answer before circling the one that most closely describes how you would react. Just respond spontaneously, as you would if the real-life situation occurred.

1. You are behind schedule in completing a project. A member of your staff enters your office with a problem. She can be extremely garrulous, and usually her problems aren't serious ones. You can solve most in a few minutes. Would you:

    a. Cut her off, tell her you are too busy today to talk, then get back to work?

    b. Put aside the work and listen to her problem, then solve it for her?

    c. Ascertain quickly if this is a crisis? If it isn't, suggest you meet after you have completed your deadline when you can both discuss the problem and you can help her identify the solution.

2. You and your staff have just completed a study of WYX-TW product. You want to write the report because you think you have identified some key issues that others might miss, but your desk is stacked with job-required paperwork. Do you:

    a. Put aside the paperwork to write the report? After all, it has a long-term dollars value?

    b. Call the proposed recipient of the report, tell her you have some nifty insights, and ask if the report can wait a week?

    c. Have a team member draft the report after sharing your insights with her to be sure that those points would be included in the report?

3. Knowing that sales are down, you devote your time to:

    a. Calling distributors to identify problems and solutions to the fall in revenue.

    b. Reviewing economic projections about the nation's economy with an eye to preparing your variance report for the month.

    c. Calling salespeople to demand they up-perform over the next two weeks to meet the operating statement budgets.

4. You are meeting with your staff to tell them about a new customer database to be installed. As a part of your presentation, you:

    a. Point out that this system has been delayed for some time because the division has not been perceived as a moneymaking operation.

    b. Indicate that senior management recognizes the contribution your division can make and, in keeping with your department goal to identify ancillary products, is providing the department with a tool to help both marketing and product managers improve product targeting.

    c. Inform your staff that they are lucky to get the system, explaining why, and accordingly add that you hope they will use it.

5. The designer of a new product's package has provided you with mechanicals for the package. When your boss, Sam, stops by, you show it to him and his immediate reaction is lukewarm. You:

    a. Relay his reaction to the designer: "Sam really doesn't like this. You'll have to come up with a new design."

    b. Ask Sam to explain his reaction, and he says the design doesn't lend itself to plans the firm has for marketing in another area of the operation. You then take careful notes to share with the designer later.

   c. Ask Sam to explain his reaction and he says, "I like the design but tell the designer to use some other kind of graphics on the cover of the package." You don't press him for specific examples of the graphics he has in mind or the marketing to accomplish. When you talk to the designer, you quote Sam and rush on to another appointment.

6. Management is encouraging each department to operate as a team. To encourage an attitude of teamwork in your operation, you:
   a. Talk to each member of your department about the value of teamwork and hold a stand-up meeting to extol the values of closer staff working relationships.
   b. Hold monthly staff meetings at which members of the group describe activities they are engaged in, share successes and failures, and recognize the accomplishments of individual members.
   c. Send a memo to the staff reminding them they are all members of a team and that you expect them to pull together no matter what their own job responsibilities are.

7. One of your staff members is new in the department and ambitious. She has been asking for a chance to work on her own account from the beginning. You assign her an account:
   a. It is, however, one of the toughest clients you have. This will teach her that she is too inexperienced to take on a client of her own.
   b. You thereafter accompany her on all meetings with clients, whom you pitch to show her how it is done.
   c. You thereafter monitor her progress, setting up weekly reviews over the short term to be sure everything is going well.

8. Your new salesperson gets angry at a client and blows up at him. You:
   a. Blow up at her in turn. After all, this is a valuable client.
   b. Sit down and discuss damage control with her. You cover not only how to solve the client's problem but how to handle the blowup and how to prevent it from happening again. You point out what she did right as well as wrong.
   c. Avoid her because you are too angry to calmly discuss the situation. When the client calls, you apologize and reassign him to another staff member. Only later does the new salesperson find out about the change—at the network printer (today's water cooler).

9. Your company has just implemented a new procedure for processing customer orders. You:
   a. Draft a memo describing the procedure and circulate it to your staff.
   b. Draft a memo describing the procedure, then hold a meeting at which you review it in detail, answer questions related to it, and

discuss how it could be improved. Ideas generated at the meeting are shared with senior management.

c. Hold a stand-up meeting with your staff at which you describe the new procedure.

10. You are head of public relations in an organization that has in place a new total quality management effort aimed at improving product quality. To reflect this new concern about quality within your department, you:

   a. Do nothing because you already know your task. It is to tell the press how well your company's TQM program works.

   b. Hold a series of meetings of staff members to apply the TQM effort to public relations, pinpointing ways you can improve relations with the media.

   c. Joke about the program with staff members, saying, "It's just another fad we have to sell to the public."

11. You have an opportunity to offer an on-line service. To head up the product line, you choose:

   a. The head of New Products even though this person is a Luddite, with little interest, let alone knowledge, about on-line services.

   b. A computer whiz who would normally not be considered, given his ranking in the organization, but you feel that he has shown unusual creativity and implementation skills. And, of course, he has the computer expertise.

   c. An old pal who heads up a product group that needs a new product line to ensure no layoffs of staff.

12. Your company is looking for new products to broaden its product line. You devote much of your time to:

   a. Brainstorming with your staff to help identify market and product ideas. Once you have some good ones, you assign champions to spearhead projects to study them further.

   b. Finding opportunities to cut costs to make your department's bottom line.

   c. Day-to-day office routine, nay-saying suggestions from staff about product ideas that might distract them from their regular work.

13. Your staff member Jill has brought you information about the latest software package that would make her job easier. She suggests that the software could even be placed on your network system, which means all your staff could benefit from its use if they were as knowledgeable about the new technology as Jill. You:

   a. Agree to install the software after reviewing its benefits, then ask Jill to put together a training program to help other staffers become as skilled with it as she is.

    b. Turn down the suggestion. You know that you will lose some productivity over the short term and that could be too costly even with the longer-term time savings.

    c. Agree to consider the idea, but you are very busy and forget to take the material home that night. It gets mislaid, and the software is never installed.

14. A client makes some last-minute changes on the product your department provides. There is no way you can deliver on time through your standard production methods. You decide to:

    a. Hand-produce sufficient items to ensure final delivery of a quality product even though you must absorb the additional cost.

    b. Cut corners to ensure that the product will be delivered on schedule within budget.

    c. Tell the client that he will be to blame for any delays in delivery and that he should accept a substandard product this time out because of the process time wasted due to his perfectionism.

15. You receive a call from a service firm that is offering a more customer-sensitive way for your organization to handle accounts payable. You're not in Finance; you're in Marketing. There is no one heading up Customer Service right now, but you know that late-paying customers have complained about the attitude of those from Finance who have called about late bills. You:

    a. Recognize that this has nothing to do with you, tell the individual that he should call in about a month when the firm has a person to head up Customer Service, and hang up.

    b. Contact Finance and suggest that its head and you meet with the individual to investigate his service. The new system would mean his accountants would no longer have to handle these calls, and you both could begin studying the idea so a plan might be ready for consideration by the time a head of Customer Service is hired.

    c. Explain that it isn't your area of involvement, say, "Thank you for calling," and hang up.

16. Because of a reorganization, you are now in charge of two operations at different corporate locations, in addition to the operation at headquarters. To manage your new span of control, you:

    a. Stay in touch with your new areas of responsibility via e-mail and visits once a month to the department heads.

    b. Have each department head submit monthly reports to you that outline all events. You supplement this with quarterly visits to each facility during which you meet with the department head and participate at holiday parties.

    c. Use e-mail, monthly visits, and bimonthly staff meetings with both departments to familiarize yourself with department issues and become familiar with staff feelings as well as their supervisors'.

17. You need to increase revenue. One way you can do that is to increase purchase price on your firm's antivirus program product. At a meeting you announce the plan. Your sales manager objects, suggests several alternate approaches, and cites several reasons why a price increase will kill sales. You:

    a. Interrupt the sales manager, tell him you've thought about the situation and believe this is the only real option available, and go on with the meeting.

    b. Suggest the sales manager put his objections and alternatives in writing, knowing that you have already given marketing an OK to increase price.

    c. Listen to the sales manager's arguments and agree to hold the price for several months while you explore the alternative options suggested to increase sales channels and improve bottom line.

18. You have looked over the operating reports for the last six months. Sales are down. You suspect a problem with the product. Marketing blames it on the economy. You're not sure. As product manager, you decide to:

    a. Accept Marketing's explanation for the falloff in sales and await a return to higher sales in the spring.

    b. Conduct your own small customer survey to determine if customer needs have changed.

    c. Do a written customer survey but also bring together a group of customers to see if the exchange of information might identify reasons for the falloff in sales.

19. At the first meeting of your cross-functional group, you:

    a. Get immediately to work identifying ways to resolve the problem and implement the solution.

    b. Discuss the mission of the group, using the discussion to clarify the group's goals.

    c. Clarify your role as head of the team since you came up with the initial idea, make assignments to research your idea further, and get to work.

20. As a team leader, your most important responsibility would be to:

    a. Define the team's mission and its goals so it stays on that track through completion of the project.

    b. Complete the project on time and on budget.

    c. Ensure that each team member fully participates in the discussion.

21. To ensure a good team effort, as team leader you may have to:

a. Facilitate group discussions, encouraging members to participate and intervening when members interrupt or display poor team-member behavior.

b. Come prepared with several good ideas to help the group get started at brainstorming.

c. Maintain control of the discussion so it moves in the direction you want the group finally to take.

22. You are leading a cross-functional team when two team members, Harold and Marvin, get into an argument over Marvin's idea for solving a problem tied to the team's mission. Harold begins to throw epithets at Marvin. You:

     a. Suggest to Harold that you want to hear Marvin's idea, then want to listen to the entire group's reaction to it, as well as other ideas for solving the problem, including Harold's.

     b. Regain control of the meeting by telling both Marvin and Harold to shut up and let others speak.

     c. Let the argument continue until other members pressure Harold and Marvin to be silent.

23. Harold and Marvin continue their argument outside the meeting room. You can hear their voices across the office floor. Your first objective is to:

     a. Get them back to their respective offices and return the work space to normal. Then you can address the problem that caused the argument.

     b. Find out who started it and discipline him for misconduct.

     c. Ignore the argument. Harold and Marvin clearly have a personality conflict that extends outside the team meeting room, and since you are not either's supervisor, their behavior, although linked to the team meeting, isn't your responsibility.

24. You are in charge of a team meeting, and one of the members questions a decision of yours, hinting you are not open to new ideas from the group. You see this as:

     a. A challenge to your leadership, so you need to put her down, which you proceed to do by responding sarcastically to her comments, making faces at her remarks, and the like.

     b. A judgment about your leadership style that you need to consider to determine how true it is. If it is, then you need to reconsider how you handle idea differences in team settings.

     c. Wrong, and disagree with her. You point this out to the group, effectively closing all further discussion on the subject.

25. One of the members of your team belittles everyone's ideas and contri-

butions. The members are no longer sharing ideas with the group because they expect to have their opinions ridiculed by this very articulate, high-level member. You:

a. Meet with him after the meeting to let him know that you appreciate his participation and ideas but that he is discouraging others from contributing to the group. If he does not stop such behavior, you will have to ask him to leave the group.

b. Allow his misbehavior to continue, trying to focus attention away from him toward the group's mission.

c. Meet privately with team members to encourage them to share their ideas regardless of his put-downs. You admit you can't control his behavior, but tell the members that you all can't allow one bad member to spoil the entire effort.

26. Conflict has arisen about whether a relatively new product should be pulled out of the market. Marketing is on the offensive, but the product group is holding its own. Others at the meeting are uncomfortable. You:

a. Call an end to the argument and make a decision based on the economic numbers submitted by Marketing, disregarding any new information about shifts in the marketplace from the product group.

b. Allow the argument to proceed, using the flip chart in the room to capture key points made by both sides. After the two seem worn out, you call everyone's attention to the points raised and attempt to reassess the situation more rationally, based on all the solid information offered.

c. Call on a member of the product group to submit a paper in favor of continuing the product, and promise to make a decision based on that report.

27. You have asked the product group to meet and put together a paper with its reasons for continuing its product line. You disagree with its stand. Once you get the report, you:

a. Distribute it along with copies of the marketing department's financials, and bring up the issue again at the next meeting: "We've given you the chance to argue your case. If anyone feels we shouldn't kill the product, please speak up."

b. Read it, then put it aside. You tell Marketing you see no point in holding off and it should proceed to kill the product.

c. Study the report and distribute it to all members of the product team for consideration. At the meeting, you put questions to both sides of the argument, then make a decision based on their replies and the entire group's input.

28. You and Stella, a creative staff member, are at a planning meeting.

Stella offers a plan to restructure the department, something that is 180 degrees away from its current mission and against your own vision for the department, yet it would give reason for the department's being at a time when sales are significantly down. You:

a. Listen respectfully to Stella's suggestion, then ask other members of the group to comment. You hold off giving your own opinion until the rest of the group has spoken.

b. React to the proposal sarcastically. You deride Stella's reputation as a workaholic, point to how her proposal would demand more staff time on ancillary efforts, and drop the idea.

c. Cut Stella off once you realize what she is about to suggest, since it is significantly different from anything you have ever considered about the group's purpose.

29. You have been at a senior staff meeting. It has been a tough morning. One of your staff members rushes over to share some good news about sales of one of the product lines she spearheads. She doesn't know that senior management has just suggested another of her products be killed. You:

a. Say, "Great. You should be really pleased with the effort." Then suggest that you both go share the results with other staff members.

b. Say, "Fine" as you rush to the sanctuary of your office.

c. Stop and hit her with the bad news about her other product. "Why should I be the only one to suffer here?" you think as you settle yourself in the chair in your office.

30. One of your employees, Bob, thinks he has the answer to a recurring operational problem. But he may be wrong, and if he is, it will cost you both time and money, since you will have to hire a temp to fill his shoes while he tests out his idea. It may also mean a delay on some other projects as well. You decide to:

a. Thank Bob for his idea but tell him that you doubt it would work and ask him to focus on his more tangible responsibilities for now.

b. Give Bob the go-ahead to test the idea but suggest he bring together a group of coworkers to help resolve any implementation problems that might crop up. Rather than pay for a temp, you go to a colleague to see if he has a staff member who can fill in for Bob while he is testing his idea.

c. Take the idea to senior management to get approval to investigate the idea. This way if it fails, you aren't the only one responsible for giving the idea a go-ahead for testing.

31. You have built a team of top-notch technicians to revise your company's TGI-124 hardware. You lack the technical background so you had to

bring the very best to bear on the problem with the component. But the effort seems stalemated. Each member has an idea on how to pursue the problem, but no consensus seems to be growing. Each member wants to work on his or her plan. You:

a. Hold off problem solving and schedule the group for some team training, even though it will cause the group to be late in making its recommendations to management. You feel this will help the members appreciate the importance of cooperation and create a climate in which they can reach consensus on some idea.

b. Have all the members prepare white papers supporting their approach, then take the papers to an expert in the field whom you know well to get his suggestion on how to proceed. You then submit your action plan to the group.

c. Choose that idea that will allow your organization to improve the product's quality, albeit at a somewhat higher cost, and make assignments to individual team members so the group's final recommendations will be submitted on schedule.

32. Steve is your peer but he is also a member of a team assembled to identify a new addition to the firm's product line. You and Steve haven't always agreed on everything, but since he was asked to join your team you and he don't seem to be able to agree on anything, both in and outside of team meetings. You:

a. Invite Steve to lunch and during lunch say, "Steve, you and I have worked well together in the past although we haven't always agreed on issues. I wouldn't want anything I've said or done during recent team meetings to destroy that solid relationship. Is there a problem I am unaware of?"

b. Avoid Steve. He obviously has some problem either at home or in the office that is putting him in a foul mood. Better to let him alone until he is his old self.

c. Discuss the matter with members of the team in private. You all agree that Steve is just jealous of the fact that you, not he, were made head of the team. You all decide to ignore Steve's arguments either for or against an idea since they are colored in jealousy.

33. You and Steve have talked about the problem developing between you. Steve feels that you are giving short shrift to his knowledge about the product area and has asked to be allowed to withdraw from the team. You:

a. Reconsider your behavior to determine if Steve has cause for his complaint. While you don't think you have unfairly treated his ideas, you can see how he might have gotten that impression, and you ask him to stay. You more closely monitor your reaction to his ideas to avoid further misunderstandings.

b. Accept his resignation.

c. Allow him to resign even though you will lose his input during team discussions, but ask him to work on a project he can do on his own that is related to the team effort to demonstrate that you respect his judgment.

34. The team has developed several ideas for a new product. Now you are ready to choose the idea you want to pursue. You:

a. Review the reports from marketing and benchmarking data on related products and choose the best idea for the group.

b. Lead the group in multivoting, eliminating ideas until the group as a whole has chosen that idea all the members agree has the best chance to succeed.

c. Conduct multivoting, ending up with an idea that, while not the "best" idea in the opinion of some members of the team, is one that *all* the members agree is likely to succeed.

35. You need a colleague's help if a study your team has put together is to work. The study requires the use of a temp to analyze the data. You have asked your colleague to lend you one of his vacant offices, but he has refused because he hopes to add to his staff shortly. You:

a. Go back to the team to see if there is some other way to get office space to accommodate the temp.

b. Probe to find out when your colleague expects to add to his staff to see if he might be amenable to your group's using the office over the short term to complete its analysis.

c. Find out when your colleague might need the office and what help he might need in the interim that your temp, if she had an office, might be able to offer him.

36. Your colleague has made available to your team the vacant office in return for your promise that the temp will be available to help his staff on some analyses it is doing. You:

a. Keep your promise, even if it means that the temp has to be paid for several extra hours of work time.

b. Tell the temp to focus all her energies on your project. After all, that is why she is there.

c. Use any free time the temp might have to help you and your own staff catch up on work you haven't completed because of time devoted to the team effort.

37. Although you promised your colleague that the temp would help his staff as well, he has refused to lend you office space to house your temp over the short term. You:

a. Go over your colleague's head to get approval from your mutual boss to use the office.

b. Ignore your colleague's refusal and place your temp in the vacant office despite his protests. After all, it *is* vacant.

c. Go back to the team to see if some member of the team has some pull with the colleague to see if you can't still make a deal.

38. Your organization has decided to install some new office technology. Your department could be the test site. You:

a. Agree for your department to be the site because you believe the technology could speed the time in which orders are processed.

b. Accept the offer because you think it is politically wise to do so. But problems encountered in the short term cause you to question your decision. You are very vocal about the problems.

c. Pass because you don't want the flow of work interrupted even if installation of the equipment could speed it.

39. A staff member who has proven his reliability in the past six years he has worked for you, has a nonwork problem: He needs to be home to take delivery on a new piece of furniture. He asks to work at home for one day, rather than take the time off as vacation. You:

a. Refuse. Although this employee is reliable and could do the work at home, you don't want to set a dangerous precedent.

b. Agree that the employee can work at home but insist that he show you the work he did the following morning.

c. Agree, trusting the employee to fulfill his part of the bargain.

40. You have just hired a part-time worker to help you during the summer months, when many members of your staff will be out of the office. At the start of her first day, you:

a. Spend a few minutes outlining her tasks, then leave her to get to work. You check her work periodically but otherwise have few discussions.

b. Spend time reviewing her work, then take her on a tour of the office, introducing her to those individuals with whom she will be working. At the end of the day, you go over her work with her, review her performance, and listen as she discusses any problems she has encountered in doing the work.

c. Delegate supervision of her to one of your staff members. It allows this employee to learn supervisory skills and frees you to focus on more critical matters.

41. Margaret, who is in Accounts Payable, has an ailing mother and consequently would like to telecommute rather than work in the office. You know that the staff likes her and would like you to help her with her

personal problem. Before you make your decision, you approach Margaret's workstation to see what equipment she might need at home. Margaret is chatting with some friends. As they leave, she begins to stare into space, oblivious to the large stack of unpaid bills on her desk. Her computer screen is dark. From your observations, you decide to:

a. Reject her request but you send her to your firm's employee assistance program personnel to see if they can point the way to some help in caring for her mother.

b. Agree to the request, purchasing a computer to allow her to work at home.

c. Agree to a trial period to determine if telecommuting will work for both of you.

42. You have just been given another assignment by the executive to whom you report. Now you have five major tasks due next week, plus three meetings to attend that may require some preparation time. You:

a. Examine each task, breaking it down into subgoals, then set completion dates for each component of the larger task.

b. Begin with the easiest task, complete it, then go on to the next most difficult, leaving the toughest assignments for last. You take paperwork for the meetings home to be perused.

c. Delegate the routine or mundane tasks to your staff, retaining high-profile tasks for yourself.

43. A colleague has asked you for help to complete a project. Your desk is piled with work. You know you don't have time to help. You:

a. Agree. You know you won't be able to help but refusing could be politically unwise in an organization that encourages managerial cooperation.

b. Say no. You explain your own situation.

c. Say no but ask if one of your staff members might be able to help either by freeing one of your colleague's employees to help your colleague or by directly helping your colleague.

44. You are in a brainstorming meeting. In past meetings one of the team has come up with more flaky ideas than solid ones, but once in a while has hit the bull's-eye with the perfect solution. You:

a. Encourage everyone to throw ideas at you and record all of them, including those you think are outrageous. After all, you never know.

b. Write on the flip chart only those ideas that you think have a chance to succeed, in essence making some managerial judgments about what is feasible and what isn't.

c. Tune out the flake. The odds of her coming up with something good are minimal, and there are some sound ideas coming from the rest of the group that should resolve the problem.

45. You have granted a staff member's request to set up a self-managed team to undertake research that might identify new spinoff products. The team has just been formed. Now you:
    a. Ignore the team. It will come back to you when it needs help, you believe. After all, you have other priorities.
    b. Meet with the team on the first day and encourage the members' initiative, wish them well, and tell them you await their finished report.
    c. Alert the individual who came to you that you want to be kept informed of team progress. You attend the first session and a few sessions as the group progresses, providing advice. When the team is ready to submit its report, you sit in on the planning process and help in developing the final proposal, which will require approval from those above you.

46. You have just been told by a colleague, who heads Department A, that one of your employees has not completed some work essential to that department. When you meet with the underperformer, he points to the lack of available information from Department B as the cause. You:
    a. Call the head of Department B to complain that its failure to provide critical information has caused a problem for you and another area of the organization.
    b. Meet with the head of Department B to determine the cause of the problem in delivering information promptly to your staff member, then brainstorm with the manager to identify a way to prevent the problem from recurring.
    c. Call the employee to task for failing to alert you to the situation, tell him it is up to him to get the information to the client department (regardless of the failure of another group to provide the information), and indicate that this problem will be a black mark on his appraisal.

47. You are in a planning meeting. Your boss is there with you. As ideas for new business opportunities are identified, you write them on a flip chart. Later, the group looks on with shock as your boss begins to cross out some of the items listed without explanation. You:
    a. Stand silently by, too intimidated to speak. The other participants follow your example.
    b. Politely ask your boss to let the group know the reasons for his deletions. You explain that knowing why these ideas aren't worthy of further consideration will help the group to have better insights into the division's plans.
    c. Meet later with your boss to discuss his decisions. He tells you why

he does not want to pursue the ideas at this time. You decide that since planning is over your staff has no need to know why your boss took the action he did.

48. During planning, the group identified twenty ideas for new products. You and your marketing department review these and choose four for follow-up. You:

   a. Distribute a report on the planning process that lists only the four final product ideas with no explanations about where the other sixteen went.

   b. Include an explanation in the report about how the decision was made to limit staff time to four projects.

   c. Meet with the staff immediately after your meeting with Marketing to review the decisions reached, ask for further input about these conclusions, and adjust them accordingly.

49. You have just discovered you are not on the invitation list of a major meeting of senior executives you have always attended. At this meeting, plans are made for the upcoming year for a group of your own team services. You:

   a. Determine through your internal network why the decision was made to exclude you from the meeting.

   b. Call the person sponsoring the meeting to determine if and why you are excluded. You point out that your group can't be responsive to her group's needs unless you know as soon as possible what those needs might be.

   c. Show up anyway; after all, it is probably just an error that you weren't notified about the meeting.

50. You have just hired a staff member. On paper, with one or two exceptions, he will be ready to go to work from the first day on the job. On the day he reports to work, you:

   a. Set him to work immediately after a brief orientation, introducing him to fellow staff members and showing him the route to the bathroom, copier and fax machines, and accounting department.

   b. Spend time, during the orientation, reviewing your plans to train him in those areas where he lacks either experience or skills, then introduce him to some staff members, individuals he may need to know to do some tasks you plan to assign him, locations of critical areas, and someone to go to for help when he has a problem.

   c. Sit him down with an annual report and other documents to read. Explain that you want him to orient himself to the organization's needs. Tomorrow or the next day, he will be busy enough.

Now compare your responses to the responses given in the next chapter. Refer to the competency references to help strengthen your skills in any areas where you honestly might have reacted differently from what management would demand.

2

How Do You Rate?

Let's see how well you did in our test. Remember, critical to the use of the test is that you respond to the hypothetical situations with a decision as you would at the moment they arose in real life, not after slowly weighing them. After all, none of us has the luxury of being able to stop a situation sufficiently long as we puzzle out what would be the best managerial response.

What we are trying to do here is identify those areas where you might react incorrectly on the spur of the moment. Once you are aware of a managerial skill need, then you are more likely to think before you act. After a while, the right reaction should become second nature.

Below are the correct responses with an explanation for each. We have provided numbers, in parentheses, to enable you to identify the pertinent competencies in the Core Competency Checklist in the Appendix at the back of the book. The Checklist is organized so that you can easily find the chapter that deals with a specific competency in order to increase your strength in that area.

1. No matter how busy you may be, you should not be rude to a staff member who is interested in talking to you. Answer *a* is clearly incorrect, and most managers know that. Answer *b* resolves the problem but doesn't give the employee an opportunity to learn from the experience. Answer **c** describes what a high-value manager would do. It represents a smarter use of time and reflects a willingness to actively listen to an employee's concern and help her develop her skills. (See core competencies 2, 5, and 68.)

2. The correct answer is **c.** You might think that only you can do justice to the report, but that's unlikely. Asking for a delay might give you the personal satisfaction of doing the report, but it won't help you to develop one of your team members. Which is what empowering him or her to write the report will do. (See core competencies 1, 8, and 16.)

3. A high-value manager is more interested in identifying the source of the problem and solving it. So the correct answer is **a.** Answer *b* and *c* might protect you or turn around the numbers over the short term, but they are unlikely to get to the root cause of the falloff, and thereby to ensure healthy sales figures in the future. (See core competencies 2, 22, and 23.)

4. You want to motivate your staff. Neither answer *a* nor *c* does that. Answer **b** leaves your staff feeling positive about the future and their ability to influence it. It's the response of a high-value manager. (See core competencies 3 and 4.)

5. Answer **b** allows your designer to better understand what you and your boss want the package design to convey. Answer *a* tells the designer only that Sam doesn't like what he saw, it doesn't help him come up with a new design. Answer *c* is no better help since it still fails to give the designer a clear idea of what Sam wants the package to look like. A high-value manager listens actively and probes to get insights into the reasons why. (See core competencies 2 and 23.)

6. Answers *a* and *c* encourage a sense of teamwork. Answer **b** demonstrates team spirit, and it is what a high-value manager does. It's fine to talk teamwork but more difficult to practice it, and that's what a high-value manager does in bringing his or her group together to share successes and failures. (See core competencies 2, 4, 7, and 39.)

7. Answer **c** demonstrates how a high-value manager develops a talented newcomer. No good manager sets up an employee for failure—which is what answer *a* is all about—no matter how hard it is to supervise the individual. Answer *b* only allows you to showcase your own ability. (See core competencies 4, 5, and 10.)

8. Highly coveted managers may lose their temper; after all, we're all human. But losing one's temper won't help improve client relations or your salesperson's ability to deal with difficult people or situations. So answer *a* is incorrect. Answer *c* is also incorrect: Although it might rebuild good customer relations, it likely demoralizes your salesperson. Answer **b** is the correct answer. Your objective here should be twofold: to salvage customer relations and a newcomer who may need some training on how to stay calm during heated moments. (See core competencies 4, 5, 26, 27, and 28.)

9. Answer **b** makes best use of the experiences of the staff. Answer *a* only ensures that a memo is circulated; it doesn't even guarantee that the memo gets read. Answer *c* communicates the new procedure but it

doesn't get buy-in to the procedure by the department. Asking staff for their suggestions, and passing these ideas along to senior management, tells staff that you value their ideas. Even if all aren't included in the new procedures, the new procedures are more likely to be followed because the staff feels that they played a part in their creation. (See core competencies 1, 2, 4, 7, and 8.)

10. Answer **b** is the correct one. Total quality doesn't end on the plant floor. It's a program that should extend throughout the organization, as high-value managers recognize. Ignoring the program or, worse, joking about such an initiative sends a message to staff that TQM is this month's fad, which it certainly isn't. (See core competencies 26, 27, 28, and 29.)

11. High-value managers know the strengths and weaknesses of their staff. They aren't concerned about job titles. Rather, they are concerned about results. Answer **b,** our computer whiz, would be best qualified to head up the product line. Answer *c* is clearly the wrong one; high-value managers never allow friendships to influence their decisions. Answer *a* would mean the failure of the new product line—although a high-value manager might want to coach the head of New Products and follow coaching up with an assignment as a member of the new products team headed by his computer whiz. The new products manager will learn about this latest technology, and the computer whiz will develop some team leadership skills. So getting them to work together might be beneficial for both. (See core competencies 1, 8, 16, and 18.)

12. A high-value manager focuses his or her time and attention on corporate goals. Answer *b* saves money but it doesn't have the longer-term benefits of having more products producing income. Nay-saying suggestions from staff—*c*—ignore the corporate focus. Answer **a** focuses staff attention in the direction of growth, the direction senior management has identified. (See core competencies 4, 12, 21, and 23.)

13. Answer **a** is correct. It takes advantage of the new technology, plus gives Jill the chance to demonstrate her abilities and train the rest of the staff—all to the benefit of the organization, since the package over the longer term will lead to higher productivity. Answer *b* is a short-term view. Answer *c* suggests that you aren't interested in technology's applications. While it's easy to forget to follow through on some staff request, a high-value manager would go back to Jill for another copy of the information and investigate its potential. (See core competencies 8, 19, 21, and 76.)

14. A high-value manager demonstrates his or her commitment to quality service or product. Answer **a** is clear evidence that you mean what you say. Answers *b* and *c* show that in your view "total quality management" are meaningless words. (See core competencies 12 and 29.)

15. The correct answer is **b.** You recognize that no one is responsible for the area, but you take the initiative to install a system that could improve customer relations. (Right now, these late-paying customers may be in trouble, but as the economy improves they may stay with you because you handled their accounts with tact and diplomacy.) Answer *c* does nothing to eliminate your firm's customer service problem. Communicating information that might encourage the caller to try again—answer *a*—is somewhat better but still inadequate. (See core competencies 12, 29, 30, 31, 32, and 34.)

16. You would need to do more than visit monthly to understand your new responsibilities. Likewise, attendance at holiday gatherings or special events. Answer **c** is the correct one. High-value managers spend time not only with the supervisors who report to them. They find time for gauging staff feelings as well. (See core competencies 1, 2, and 15.)

17. Answer *a* demonstrates an unwillingness to listen to others. Answer *b* will only demoralize the sales manager when he learns—and he will—that you had no intention of reconsidering your decision. The correct answer **c** recognizes the insights into the marketplace that the sales manager brings to the issue. If you had no intention of involving others in the decision, then why hold a meeting in the first place? (See core competencies, 2, 5, 7, and 42.)

18. That falloff in sales may be due to the economy, but then it could be something else. Besides, even in bad times you should be looking for ways to increase profits. Answer *b* goes toward finding a solution but **c,** the correct answer, allows you to benefit not only from a written survey but from talking with customers about their use of the product—there may be some performance problems. And there is always the possibility that in the course of the discussion other ideas may arise that will enable you to better sell the product or identify related products for your marketplace. (See core competencies 22, 23, and 26.)

19. Answer **b** is the correct answer. Answer *a* is unwise. Too often teams address symptoms, not root causes. Answer *c* suggests you never needed a real team in the first place. Its purpose is to allow you to use the expertise of others in your organization to complete a project important to your department.

20. All three of these objectives are important. Most important, however, is staying on track to achieve the group's mission and goals once they have been identified—answer **a**. (See core competencies 12, 39, and 40.)

21. As team leader, you don't dominate the team as it brainstorms ideas or discusses the situation (answers *b* and *c*). However, as answer **a** states, you do facilitate group discussion, encouraging members to participate, intervening when members display poor team behavior. (See core competencies 40, 41, and 45.)

22. Answer **a** is correct. In this instance, you are using your facilitating skill to encourage an open exchange of ideas. Answer *b* shuts up both Marvin and Harold, which isn't what you want to do. You want both to share their ideas with the group, just not disrupt the flow of discussion. Where conflict between team members has arisen, there are instances in which you might wait to intervene because you see progress coming from the heated discussion. But name calling and similar behavior only make members uneasy about contributing their own opinions. (See core competencies 40, 41, and 44.)

23. Your first goal should be to return circumstances to normal. That means separating the two feuding managers—answer **a**. It's immaterial who started the argument this time (*b*). Clearly you can't ignore the conflict, even though these individuals aren't your direct reports, since the situation is likely to impede team progress until it is resolved (*c*). (See core competencies 45, 47, and 48.)

24. Answer **b** may be the toughest of the three responses, but it is also the correct one. High-value managers recognize that they aren't always right and they are willing to listen to others, even others' feedback about their management or leadership style. You might not allow the discussion to continue, but a one-on-one after the team session is clearly called for to air the member's feelings about your receptivity to new ideas. (See core competencies 2, 45, and 49.)

25. You need to confront the team member whose behavior is making everyone uncomfortable—answer **a**. Ignoring it could put an end to real member participation and idea development (*b*). Answer *c* is a cop-out. It tells the team you lack leadership ability, and that could seriously influence their own behavior. After all, if one person can get away with violating team guidelines, then why can't they? (See core competencies 40, 41, 45, 46, 47, and 48.)

26. Here's a case where disagreement may prove fruitful; if kept under control, it may lead to a better assessment of the situation—so an-

swer **b** is best. Answer *c* might give you new insights into the situation, but it takes the decision out of the hands of the team as a whole. Answer *a* suggests you have no interest in new facts or information; you've made the decision for the team, which is not how a high-value manager builds a strong sense of team among different disciplines. (See core competency 42.)

27. Answer *a* only goes through the motions of considering an alternative approach. Answer *b* takes the decision out of the hands of the team, which tells members that your approach to team is influenced by what is under discussion. Answer **c** demonstrates a commitment to team process. (See core competencies 1, 2, 21, 44, and 47.)

28. Answer **a** is the correct one. If you want to get the full benefits of your staff's ideas, you sometimes have to listen to opinions that are 180 degrees different from your own. You also have to be willing to consider changing your own opinion when staff members can demonstrate that it may be wrong. Answers *b* and *c* show little respect for a staff member's views. (See core competencies 2, 41, 45, 47, and 49.)

29. Answer **a** is correct. A high-value manager gives recognition when it is due. Later you will need to share with the staff member the bad news. Telling her the downside immediately (*c*) deprives her of enjoying her moment of triumph. Answer *b* acknowledges a good job, but consider how you might feel if you did something you considered outstanding and someone told you, "You did fine." (See core competencies 4, 15, and 21.)

30. Answer **b** is correct. The high-value manager is not adverse to risk. The return is well worth the cost. If a colleague can lend a hand during the interim, the test won't cost anything. Advising Bob to seek others to work with in the project not only increases the chances of the idea's working but also gives him some leadership experience and a chance to network throughout the organization. (See core competencies 21, 26, 56, and 62.)

31. Answer *b* may solve this problem but it doesn't create the kind of environment in which the team can work productively together. Answer **a** both solves the problem and helps the members develop the skills for productive teamwork. Answer *c* eliminates the advantages of bringing together a group of experts to address the problem. (See core competencies 52 and 53.)

32. Answer **a** clears the air, which is critical. Answer *b* is a wait-and-see approach that is based on hope that the problem will disappear. As

high-value managers know, it might not—and it could get worse. If the team wasn't divided in loyalties before, answer *c* would assure it would be. (See core competencies 41 and 49.)

33. Answer **a** is the correct one. Answer *b* eliminates your problem but loses you the insights into the situation that Steve might bring. Answer *c* may contribute to the team's final recommendations, but it also does more to demonstrate to the rest of the team how "fair" you are than to resolve the problem between you and Steve or help the team as a whole benefit from his ideas. (See core competencies 2, 42, 43, 44, and 45.)

34. Both *b* and **c** are correct, but answer **c** is more reasonable. It's unlikely that you will get unanimity in any decision making about which ideas to pursue. The best you can hope for is to reach consensus. Answer *a* takes the decision making out of the hands of the team and places it squarely in your own. Understand that there is nothing wrong with this provided that the plan was shared initially with the team when you first met. (See core competencies 22, 23, and 24.)

35. Answer **c** is most likely to get you the office. High-value managers know how to use the needs of the other party to get what they want. Answer *b* only gives you reason to argue over why you should have the office until your colleague has his full-time staffer. Answer *a* is just giving up before you have tried. (See core competencies 56 and 57.)

36. Answer **a**, though more costly to you, is the correct one. You want to maintain your credibility and that means keeping your promises, no matter what the cost. (See core competencies 58 and 59.)

37. Neither *a* nor *b* is correct. You don't play negative politics or push a colleague out of the way if you want to be able in the future to have collegial support on other endeavors. Rather, this is the time to go back to the team to reconnoiter. Determine if a member of the team has some pull with the colleague or maybe knows what he or she might need that you could provide in return for use of the office—answer **c**. (See core competencies 58, 59, and 72.)

38. The correct answer is **a**. The high-value manager would see this as an opportunity to solve a business problem while updating the department's technology. Answer *b* has you accepting Systems' offer but for the wrong reason. And whining about the problems encountered isn't going to build good political ties with Systems or encourage them to come to your department again to test out some other technological marvel. Refusing (*c*) is clearly wrong. (See core competencies 19 and 20.)

39. Answer **c** is correct. You have worked long enough with the individual to know that he will work at home as promised. Showing under-

standing about employee situations is how high-value managers motivate their employees. (See core competency 18.)

40. Answer *c* does allow you to help develop the skills of a staff member. But it doesn't give you all the benefits that would come about by personally devoting some time as well to the part-timer's introduction into your workplace. So the correct answer is **b**, but maybe you would ask one of your staff members to oversee the work, thereby getting the added advantage of helping to grow a would-be manager's supervisory skills. (See core competency 17.)

41. You decide to reject her request but speak to the company's EAP to identify public services that could help her care for her mother—answer **a**. A trial period would give her a chance to prove she was productive, but it would be expensive and would not be representative of how she might work on a steady basis. Her work habits suggest that she would have a difficult time concentrating on work while at home. (See core competencies 18 and 20.)

42. Answer **a** is correct. While delegating some of the tasks to staff is a good idea, your selection should be based on that work your staff can best handle, not on which tasks you dislike or will bring the greatest glory to you. So answer *c* is incorrect. Beginning with the easiest task helps some people get started, so for some answer *b* might actually be correct. But high-value managers prioritize tasks by importance and work on the most important projects first. (See core competencies 66, 67, and 69.)

43. Answer *c* is correct. Answer *b* is preferable to *a*. It's an honest evaluation of your situation and it doesn't set up any false hopes from your associate. Being honest will do more for your political worth in the organization than being "cooperative" then failing to keep your promise. (See core competency 68.)

44. Answer **a** is correct. Sometimes the most outrageous ideas, with some fine-tuning, turn out to be perfect. Besides, in brainstorming all the ideas are recorded; no evaluation is done until all the ideas have been recorded. Answer *c* is likely to discourage ideas from any of the group since it is evident that you are dominating the brainstorming session. (See core competencies 15, 22, 23, and 24.)

45. Answer **c** is the correct one. You are more than giving approval for a group of employees to meet to hash out a problem and submit a solution. As sponsor, you have responsibility to oversee the team effort to be sure that the time spent is productive. Further, you should be available to help overcome any political obstacles the team encounters. And, most

important, your continuous interest will keep motivation high. (See core competencies 2, 4, 15, 21, 34, and 63.)

46. Time is better spent identifying the cause of the problem and eliminating the chance of its repetition. While the underperformer clearly should have alerted you to the problem in the making, and must be reminded of his need to take a more proactive approach to situations, placing blame on either the underperformer or head of the Department B won't get you anywhere (answers *a* and *c*). The correct answer is **b**. (See core competencies 1, 22, 23, and 34.)

47. Answer **b** is correct. While *c* will provide the same information, it is better when shared with the group—and the most productive time to share that information is while you are in planning. (See core competencies 1, 4, 5, and 15.)

48. While you and marketing may have made the right decisions, you both may benefit at this stage from the input of the planning group as a whole. So answer **c** is best. It still allows changes to be made, perhaps through multivoting. (See core competencies 2, 4, 15, and 25.)

49. Answer *c* might be what you would want to do, but it is politically unwise. Answer *a* may help you determine the real reason you were excluded, but it may also only reveal what the rumor mill believes was the reason. Answer **b** is best because it not only allows you to find out specifically from the person putting together the meeting why you were excluded, but also allows you to stress the importance of your participation in the meeting. (If your exclusion is a warning that your job is in danger, this is also the best way to find out.) (See core competencies 23, 72, 73, and 74.)

50. Answer **b** is correct. You need to include an assessment of the recruit's training needs and share with him your plans for immediate and longer-term training, in addition to spending time orienting him to the organization's objectives and responsibilities, its place within the total corporate mission, and so forth. No new hire should be left alone with a few pamphlets to read on the first day. It is much better to get someone to work immediately, then review that work at the end of the day to identify any misunderstandings. So answer *c* is incorrect. *A* is what most managers do. It's a start but it isn't sufficient. (See core competencies 1, 6, 8, 9, and 10.)

How well did you do? Often we know what we *should* do but don't do it because it hasn't become a part of our natural behavior. That takes time. This book is designed to help you change knee-jerk reactions to management situations to more-productive responses.

Check to see how understanding the core competency might have helped you in the situation. Understand that the core competencies are the foundations for better management, not the answers per se to any of the situations we've chosen here. These situations are real-life ones experienced by managers we interviewed. Generally, they aren't black and white; there is a lot of gray in making management choices. But the core competencies we've identified should give you the start to better understand how to grow your skills and abilities, plus change your attitude about how you work with others where change is necessary.

To help you further, we have included some questions to ask your employer or supervisor, staff member(s), clients, and colleagues. That will give you an idea of how you should go about changing your management approach.

Ask your employers:

- Am I focusing the department's attention on those issues you see as important?
- Are there problems in my department that I am unaware of?
- Are there problems in my management style that I should be aware of?
- How can I better support your efforts?

Ask your employees:

- What can I do to help you do your job?
- Does my style of management cause problems for you in doing your work? If so, what are these problems?
- How can I better use your skills and abilities?
- What problems do you think I should address in this department?

Ask your clients or customers (internal or external):

- Is my staff providing the product or services you need when you need them?
- What can we do together to see that the quality of service or products we provide meets your needs?
- What problems do you encounter when you work with my staff members? Have you any ideas how we can deal with these?

- How would you measure the quality of service we provide? What could we do to make it better?

Ask your colleagues:

- What can we do together to address problems we both share?
- Have I been supportive of your efforts? If not, what can I do?
- Are there ways that our respective staffs can work more effectively together to produce better returns?
- How would you describe our collegial relationship?

Ask yourself:

- So, how am I doing?

Understand that these are only trigger questions, designed to help you to open the door to honest communications with those who know your management skills and abilities best. Actively listening to the response is the first step to becoming a high-value manager. Which is what Sections II through V are all about.

Section II
Strategic Leadership

The highly coveted manager sees his or her role as one that is shared with members of the work group or team. More coach than manager now, the high-value manager is more leader than ever before as he or she empowers staff members to assume a greater decision-making role in the organization.

Our high-value manager brings his or her team members into the planning process, tying decisions on a departmental level to those made on the senior level. He or she creates an environment in which staff members are free to learn—to make mistakes if they learn from them—and to apply their learning in real-world situations that go beyond the requirements of their job description or their box in the organization chart.

In being a strategic leader rather than manager, the high-value manager brings to his or her group the vision and values of the organization as a whole, shares them with the group, and directs a more focused effort to achieve his or her corporation's strategic intent.

3

From Managing to Empowering

Today's organizations demand a change from traditional management. Understand: We're not at all alluding to the all-knowing, autocratic manager when we refer to traditional management. The culture and value systems of today's companies have not tolerated this kind of manager for some time. When we talk about traditional management, we are talking about managers who share responsibility through delegation but generally still oversee the work done by their staff members. Such management is no longer possible.

Leaner managerial staffs mean that those managers who survived the downsizing or rightsizing of their organizations have longer to-do lists than ever before. Many have greater spans of control. They either have absorbed into their operation responsibilities once handled by a department that no longer exists or now oversee more than one operation, even operations farther removed than a few office floors. Whichever the reason, they don't have the time they once had to look over the shoulders of their employees. Delegation is no longer sufficient to allow today's managers to "manage." They need to truly "empower" their employees.

High-value managers are coveted because they have freed themselves through empowerment to focus successfully on those parts of their managerial jobs that are critical to their organization's strategic objectives. In doing this through empowerment, they also are helping their organization to benefit from the knowledge and insights their staff members can bring to the work because they are closest to it. And in the process they are making their staff members' jobs more challenging and helping their staff members develop new skills.

As a progressive and hardworking manager, you undoubtedly know the importance of delegating responsibilities to your employees. You've made it a practice to observe your employees and give them more assignments as they develop the skills with which to handle them. However, we are now asking you to take this a significant step forward. It is time for you to learn how to share the leadership and direction of your organization with the individuals who are charged with making it happen. When you empower your employees, you give them not just tasks to do. You give them areas of responsibility and decision-making authority to deal with situations that arise daily. You move from treating your staff members as children, providing them with instruction, to interacting with them as adults in adult-to-adult communication.

Some managers see empowerment as a threat to their position. As they give decision-making power to their staffs, they worry that they make themselves dispensable. On the contrary, high-value managers have learned how sharing their power gives them the time to work on high-visibility projects, to identify and pursue opportunities for their operation or company as a whole, and consequently to increase their worth in the eyes of senior management. And, ultimately, it can lead to advancement. Indispensability may ensure you keep your current position, but it also almost guarantees that you never move beyond it. And high-value managers don't put limits on their future.

Experience has also shown that employees have greater respect for those managers who share the decision making. Managers demonstrate their self-confidence in their own position and their confidence in their employees when they empower their staff members. Loyalty grows as employees see their manager on their side.

Before you make this significant change in management style, though, you need to prepare your employees. If you introduce the concepts of shared leadership and empowerment carefully to your employees, you can avoid being hit with any confusion or resentment that might follow, particularly if your style in the past has been more traditional, even occasionally autocratic. It may even be advisable to hold a meeting in which you explain how you want to shift operating gears and management style, both for your benefit and your employees'. Admit that it's no longer possible for any one person to have all the answers or make all the decisions. Express your desire to recognize the value of each individual's contributions and knowledge. Ask for your employees' help. Those asked for help usually give it.

Certainly, the commitment to implementing shared leadership is something that you personally must make if you are going to make a change. Start by asking yourself the following questions:

1. What areas of responsibility do I currently have that I would most like to see handled by someone else?

2. What skills do my employees have that are being underused?
3. How could I better use my time if I were freed of some of the hands-on managing I do now?

Chances are, the answers to those three questions alone can get you started thinking about how empowerment can improve your department if you can win agreement with your employees. The key thing to remember about empowerment is that asking employees to take on greater responsibility does not mean you can abandon them. As manager, you should still be available to your employees for help, but with time you will find they will make more and more of these decisions on their own and also by consulting coworkers.

In order to successfully empower your employees, there are several core competencies—skills, abilities, and attitudes—you need to have. You need to:

1. Understand any new areas of responsibility and the skills and backgrounds of your new staff members to make the best people and management decisions. You need a foundation of information if you are to operate your newer, broader span of control productively and effectively through empowerment.

2. Listen actively. This involves listening both to what is said and what isn't said. Maybe even more important, it means listening to your employees' opinions and concerns with a willingness to change your own opinion. When you demonstrate active listening, you send signals about your willingness to share leadership.

3. Operate on purpose. There should be a relationship between each task you or a staff member does and the objectives or goals of your department or organization as a whole. In giving any assignments, you need to communicate that relationship. Your employees should have some understanding of how their work will affect individual departments and the company as a whole so they can make the most effective decisions possible on their own.

4. Emphasize growth and opportunity. No matter what the situation, the high-value manager attempts to present to his or her staff a picture of a glass half full, not half empty. He or she invites employees to join in sharing the leadership of a *winning* organization, one that has room for growth and development. A high-value manager doesn't ask staff members to stay aboard a sinking ship.

5. Train employees to think critically. Encourage them to examine the how, why, and what they are doing as they fulfill their work assignments. Allow them the opportunity to question how things were done in the past and to come up with new procedures, processes, or practices that will enable them to more efficiently or effectively do the work. Post-reengineering demands you become a change master. Allow your employees to become change masters as well.

1. Understand New Operations

If you have assumed new responsibilities, much of what you know may be inaccurate, based more on hearsay than operating statements. Any decisions you make might be founded more on preconceived ideas than hard facts. Likewise, you may know your new staff members from staff parties or other social events but it's unlikely you are familiar with the level of their performance or capability. Consequently, without some time spent getting to know your new employees, you may be reacting to their social skills rather than professional skills, to their reputation (which may or may not be a reflection of their abilities) rather than their capabilities.

So don't make any decisions, either about the operation or to whom to empower decisions, until you have sufficient time to understand both the management problems and the people with whom you now will work. Consider the case of Stockard:

Empowering the Wrong Employee

Stockard survived a downsizing with a new title—national sales manager. Regional sales managers were laid off, and the entire sales operation was centralized under Stockard, who now found herself responsible for four regions she knew nothing about, plus an additional twenty-five salespeople, whom she recalled meeting at past corporate conferences but otherwise was unfamiliar with. In fact, she couldn't place faces on any members of her new sales force. Since management expected sales to rise 4 to 6 percent over the next year, Stockard knew she had to move as quickly as possible to overcome the impact of the downsizing in the other sales regions and pull the five groups together as a team. Toward that, she visited each sales region and met with staff.

In the northeastern region, she was particularly impressed

with the sales records of two salespeople. They had equally impressive reputations. One, in particular, impressed Stockard. Pat had a wonderful sense of humor and seemed to know everyone in the region and company well. Jim, the other individual, had a sales record that exceeded Pat's, but he was quieter than Pat. At meetings, Jim was last to speak up, but he was also someone everyone seemed to listen to. But because Jim was so quiet, most forgot he was the individual who had tied the ideas together or come up with the better way of proceeding.

Unaware of this fact, Stockard chose to give Pat some of the key accounts because of his sales record and outgoing personality. This was a critical decision, but she thought it was well made given Pat's solid track record plus familiarity with all the companies in his region.

As the quarter passed, Stockard watched sales in each division to see if the management goal was reached. Every region except the Northeast was on track. When she visited the Northeast, she met with each salesperson personally. Jim was able to point to an increase of over 10 percent among his customers. Pat showed an increase of only 2 percent, far below what his key accounts should have contributed to the region's final numbers, but Pat had explanations and excuses that Stockard accepted.

Before leaving the area, however, she decided to visit with the former regional sales director—Nils—who now was working with a competitive firm. Nils held no hard feelings against Stockard, and over lunch he was delighted to share stories about his sales staff with her. In the retelling of some of the stories, something became evident to Stockard. Jim lacked Pat's social skills, but Nils considered Jim a better salesman. Pat was all flash, with lots of talent at shmoozing customers. He had a commendable sales record, but he needed constant supervision to buckle down—which is what Nils had provided.

Stockard hadn't been giving any of that direction to either Pat or Jim, or any of her sales force. Given her other responsibilities, she had chosen to empower her sales force. Her failure to determine who could really be empowered and who still needed some supervision was costing her company real dollars at a critical time—and could affect her position over the

longer haul. For instance, Nils told Stockard how Pat often neglected pushing new products; on the other hand, Jim's customers often came to Nils after hearing about new applications
from Jim. Nils had had to set quotas in the new-product area
to get the kind of performance from Pat that had impressed
Stockard.

What does this story tell you about empowering new staff members?
Begin slowly. Determine first their ability to be empowered before sharing major responsibility with them. In Stockard's case, she would have
been better off splitting the key accounts in the northeastern region
among the best sales personnel in that office rather than taking the risk
she did by making Pat responsible for them all. She certainly should have
visited with some of both Pat's and Jim's clients to determine and compare the respect each man had earned rather than make a decision based
on the superficial impression she got from a half hour with each staffer.
Nils's testimony indicated that—charming personality notwithstand-
ing—Jim's performance had always outshone Pat's in those areas that
were most important to the company: overall and new product sales, client retention, and travel and expenses (Pat took a lot of potential clients
to lunch with no sales results, while Jim's lunches celebrated closure on
major orders).

We've been talking about the importance of knowing your new staffers when you make empowerment decisions, but in light of greater control spans, that's not all that is important to empowerment. In creating a
culture in which empowerment may be practiced, you need to:

1. *Share your story.* At a group meeting, or in a letter to your staff,
tell them about yourself, how you came to your present position, and
your plans to empower the members of the group over time. By taking
away the mystery, you open the doors to comfortable communications,
clearer understanding, and ultimately empowerment.

2. *Ask before you act.* The culture has to support empowerment. So,
even if you have no choice in a matter, get feedback on how a change will
affect your new staff or enlarged staff group and what you can do to
make the transition smoother.

If you make changes, make them on a trial basis. It can be difficult to
predict the outcome of your proposals. So approach change on an experiential basis, leaving yourself and your employees the option of reverting
back to the old method or trying another alternative.

Most important, when announcing such changes, make public the fact that the new procedure is being tested, that you will welcome the opportunity to hear from your new staff members on how the changes affect them, and that the changes aren't cast in concrete. Adjustments will be made; practices being tested may even be discontinued if they prove unproductive.

3. *Involve staff in any changes you make.* Seek your new employees' opinions and advice and take into consideration feelings of ownership individuals may have about specific jobs. Don't treat your new staff members as instruments or tools to make the business operation run. Ask employees to submit a formal evaluation of how a proposed change would influence their performance, and share with them your evaluation of how the unit's productivity is affected. Thus any experiments in operational procedures become a means for making changes intelligently, cautiously, and even considerately.

You may choose to use a form like Figure 3-1 to solicit your employees' opinions on the new procedures.

4. *Eliminate redundant operations slowly.* You want to build support for yourself, your plans, and your goal to empower as many employees as are willing and able to be empowered.

2. Listen to Employees

What is the most active change you may have to make in order to grant empowerment to your staff members? You have to learn how to truly listen to their opinions and their concerns. The traditional manager has primarily acted in a parental role toward staff members—listening patiently perhaps, but always with the thought that he or she can solve the problem better than an employee. The high-value manager has to acknowledge that employees are intelligent and perceptive adults and that he cannot make up his mind on what action should be taken until the employee makes a case for his own plan. Even when you believe that you instinctively know what to do, your job is now to help your employees learn how to solve their own problems. You can do this by training yourself to allow them to do their own problem solving and trying to limit your contribution to guidance and advice. You can then turn your attention to higher-level matters.

We were at a meeting recently in which the team leader cut off any member of the team whose ideas moved in directions other than the one

Figure 3-1. Change evaluation form.

Name:

New Procedure

How has this change affected your work?

_____

_____

_____

Have you seen an increase in efficiency because of this change? Please explain.

_____

_____

_____

Have you seen any changes in the quality of your work or that of others?

_____

_____

_____

Have you established any new working relationships with peers/staff members/ supervisors as a result of this change?

_____

_____

_____

_____

_____

Have you discovered any problems caused by this change?

_____

_____

_____

Do you have any suggestions for improving upon this procedure?

_____

_____

Do you have any objections to making this a permanent change in procedure?

_____

_____

_____

in which the leader wanted to move. This manager's manner cast a decided color on the meeting that likely discouraged a free flow of ideas. This same manager has been known to set time and topic limits in one-on-one conversations with more garrulous staff members. Another manager holds free-flowing idea sessions every two weeks in which participants are given the opportunity to bring up any subject of concern. This manager holds her own opinions back at meetings until all the members of her work group have had the chance to voice their opinion. She doesn't want to dominate the discussion; she wants to empower the group to think for itself. Which manager would you prefer to work for? Which one is likely to truly empower his or her people and to benefit from that empowerment?

To gauge your listening skills, ask yourself these questions:

- Do I remain quiet to allow someone to finish speaking even though I disagree with what I hear? Do I hold my emotions in check as well?
- Do I listen between the lines, looking for hidden meanings and watching body language, to determine what the person is really saying?

- Do I paraphrase to ensure that I have not misunderstood what has been said?
- Do I set up meetings so I won't be distracted?
- When some member of my staff wants to speak to me, do I clear my desk and my mind to give the individual my full attention?
- If I can't pull myself away from what I am doing, do I set up a time to meet with the staff member to give him or her my full attention?

If you can answer yes to these questions, you are moving in the direction of creating a climate in which empowerment can successfully be implemented.

3. Operate on Purpose

To enable your staff members to operate as an empowered team, you must *operate on purpose*. What does that mean?

To operate on purpose, you must (1) tie all operating decisions, responsibilities, and tasks to the department vision or mission; then (2) communicate to staff members how their specific jobs and tasks relate to the group's mission or that of the company so they can make decisions in doing their work that benefits that mission. They can then be safely empowered because the decisions they make will be designed to benefit the organization.

The first step is a planning issue. You have to look at your operation in light of the company's objectives, then examine each job within the department, and each task within that job to be sure that effort is directed productively. Those tasks that do not contribute to the group or corporate mission may not need to be done at all or may be done, but only after all tasks or projects linked to corporate strategy are completed.

Let's assume, for instance, that your organization is going through a period of economic instability. The company has no interest in new products. Creative staff members are better focusing their talents on identifying ways to save money than creating new products that the company is not in a position to either develop, produce, or market. Likewise, your company has no distribution channel to produce product 2378x but you've asked one of your staff members to develop a proposal to make a product competitive with 2378x. This is poor use of the staff member's time unless your organization plans to develop the needed distribution channel.

So first you need to check your own operation to be sure that all tasks are purposeful. Then you need to focus on communicating to your employees, first, the department and corporate mission and vision and, second, the role their work will play in achieving both. For employees to be able to assume more responsibility over their job—to take on actual ownership of a goal—they need to know the reason for that goal (its place in the overall scheme of things, which may include why achievement of that goal is being done in a particular way). They need to work purposefully, and it is up to you to show them the way.

For many workers it is hard to see how their individual position either contributes to or detracts from the greater goals of the organization. It is the job of today's (and tomorrow's) manager to be able to help workers to see the connection between what they do and the corporate mission.

Give them access to information that will enable them to make the right decisions when the time comes to make them. Distribute productivity reports, progress reports, industry polls, and any other information you yourself use in keeping current on the job to all your employees— even those whose jobs do not seem to require this information. As obvious as it may be to you, point out the different departments that depend on your input and also those that help you out with support services. Name those individuals they will need to know in these operations to resolve problems that arise.

Certainly include employees in the management planning that may affect their jobs. Keep them informed. Management has always been somewhat stingy with sharing its feelings and plans, but if employees are going to be expected to give 100 percent of their effort they are going to have to be treated as equally interested parties.

4. Emphasize Growth and Opportunity

If your employees are to accept this greater role, you have to make them feel that they are a part of a winning team. That entails monitoring your own behavior and words.

In your words and actions, you need to send a clear message that the group's professionalism is respected. This creates a positive feeling within the group that reinforces their willingness to play a more active role in the group's decisions. This is especially important if your group is experiencing some tough economic times. They need to know the financial realities, but they also need to feel that the company will support financially as well as operationally good decisions that contribute to the bottom line.

You need to get your employees to view problems as opportunities to succeed and to devise new methods of doing things. Toward the latter, you might suggest employees approach problems from a "hindsight" perspective, imagining what they want to accomplish and working backwards to the best procedure to follow. But know that the kind of positive attitude about the workplace that will lead to more and better employee ideas won't come about by your telling staffers that they now have the freedom to be creative and make errors. Rather, it will be in the way you act and react to their ideas and suggestions.

The management that chooses to keep its employees in line by warning them of overspending, inefficiency, or making errors may succeed in its attempt to keep its staff very careful and cautious with company resources. However, it will also succeed in stifling its own growth, as any change requires experimentation and, as a result, some waste of time or material goods. Operating from an attitude of abundance is required of the manager who wants to see his or her department expand its responsibilities and increase its productivity.

5. Train Employees to Think Critically

Declaring employees to be empowered is easy, but actually getting them to take ownership of their work processes can be difficult. Workers often look cynically on corporate policies encouraging them to innovate. Show your employees how to think critically about how they perform tasks by initiating change yourself. Engage your staff in exploring opportunities for streamlining procedures, demonstrating that you really approve of change. Show that established procedures are not sacred so that your employees can explore opportunities to improve efficiency and quality with confidence.

It is natural for employees to be reluctant to make suggestions for change, but in an environment of shared leadership, you can gradually train employees to do so. The training process will be more successful if you:

• *Turn employees' questions back to them.* Don't be so quick to offer a solution to a problem, even when it's obvious to you. Ask the individual, "What do you think you should do?" Then listen to his answer and avoid commenting until he is finished. You may need to ask some follow-up questions in order to get the employee to think of a solution on his own.

▪ *Encourage employees to consult coworkers.* Instead of providing answers, suggest your employees ask for advice from coworkers who may have had the same situation to deal with. You may at first have to ask the coworker to help out the employee, but eventually it will help the group to work more cooperatively as a team. Help individual employees to evolve from people who do their jobs well and independently to a source of help or resident expertise for others in the department to turn to.

▪ *Meet resistance with patient persistence.* There will always be those employees who are perfectly happy with the status quo and have little interest in getting more involved. They prefer to put in an honest days' work and go home and forget about it until the next morning. However, with some persistence it is possible to win over these individuals to take on more accountability. You can encourage individuals by focusing on what they do best and asking for help from them when needed. Continue to include them in all department meetings and add responsibilities slowly so as not to overwhelm them. As each new task is accomplished, give them a lot of positive feedback and recognition. Eventually, the new order will become familiar and comfortable to them. They may never be the spark behind change for the department, but can continue to be important contributors and cooperative team members.

4

Providing a Learning Environment

If staff members are to share in the leadership of work groups or departments, they will need skills that go beyond those they have today. The high-value manager works with them to help them develop these—both the decision-making and the job skills they will need to become a productive part of their company's value chain.

Interestingly, we have observed that the most talented and valuable of staff members often don't get the training they need to grow because their managers are reluctant to allow them the time away from the office or plant to get the training. The manager considers their contribution to be so valuable that they can't be spared the time away from the job.

As a high-value manager, you know better. You recognize the importance of training particularly to your most talented staff members. You find ways to free them from the day-to-day routine to allow them time off to advance their skills and increase the contribution they can make to your organization.

In this period of tremendous change, the high-value manager sees learning as critical and consequently creates an environment in which it is continuous. It is understood that as staff members take on greater responsibilities mistakes will occur, but it is also hoped that staff will learn from these mistakes. And the organization as a whole will profit as its human assets grow in value from taking on ever challenging projects and tasks with minimal supervision.

To create a true learning environment, the high-value manager must:

6. Undertake during the job interview a training needs assessment that is pursued if the individual is hired.

7. Structure work groups so members can share their knowledge and skills with one another. From the sharing should come learning.

8. Monitor on-the-job training. Informal learning should be consistent with the job, customer service, and quality standards that the department or organization has set.

9. Practice action learning. Classroom instruction is not enough. The manager must lead the group as it learns from working on real-life problems.

10. Be willing to take on the role of teacher. Managers must take on some of the formal training tasks for their department.

6. Conduct Training Assessments

When we interview candidates for staff positions, we often recognize deficiencies in their skills. Even the individual we finally hire may lack certain skills that are necessary for the job or for some plans we have for their new role. Yet often when the person begins to do the job, we forget those gaps in experience or learning that we recognized during the hiring stage.

High-value managers take written note of deficiencies during the hiring process so they can refer to this information on the recruit's first day on the job. As a part of the orientation, they identify specific training objectives over either the short or long term to better enable the employee to fulfill his or her new responsibilities. This starts the employee off more positively in his or her new job.

Together with the recruit, the high-value manager sets up a list of goals for the first month and beyond. They discuss what the employee will be expected to do, who will teach the employee the job, and how the high-value manager and the employee expect performance to evolve over the next few months. The employee should be given real assignments from the first day, but you may want to start with relatively easy ones. If so, explain this to the new recruit. Let him or her know that the work will get more challenging as he or she becomes more knowledgeable and skilled about each task.

If the gaps are important, then you might want to arrange for the recruit to attend a formal training course before starting to perform his or her duties. When the employee checks in, you can explain the need for this training and its importance to success on the job.

The job description is the basis for making the training needs assessment. Where the individual's resume suggests gaps in experience or skills to perform job requirements, then these need to be noted. The better written the job description, the easier it is to identify these gaps. The secret to a well-written job description is the use of active verbs that specify behaviors essential to job performance—verbs like "construct," "list", "prepare," "produce." Verbs like "observe," "understand," "appreciate," or "identify" make it difficult to evaluate performance during an appraisal interview as well as to conduct a training needs assessment.

The needs assessment answers two questions:

1. Why does the recruit need the training?
2. What specific training will the new hire require to do the job well?

The new hire is more responsive to the need for training if the manager can be specific in answering these two questions.

While we have suggested that training needs assessment should begin at the point of hire, note that high-value managers conduct training assessments on an ongoing basis as the department undergoes changes that demand new or better skills from its staff members. They recognize that training is continuously needed to keep the department competitive with the departments of competing firms. Otherwise, the department cannot contribute to the organization's strategic goals.

Looking beyond the present, you might develop an inventory of all the skills your staff will require, then identify those individuals who are deficient in some or all of these areas. Certainly there will be technical skills that will need upgrading. But training to improve problem-solving and decision-making skills may also be required as you endeavor to empower your staff members.

In doing a training needs assessment, here are some starting questions to ask about an employee with a performance problem—whether a recruit or a long-term worker—whose answers might lead you to believe that the problem can be solved with training:

- Has the individual received less training in X than coworkers? (If a performance problem does not seem to be due to a discipline situation and the answer to this question is yes, then you may have identified the source of the problem.)
- What changes have occurred in the workplace that would affect the way staff members work? If new technology has been introduced, have the employees had sufficient training on this equipment? Do they need more?
- How has the employee handled his or her work in the past? In

the case of a seasoned worker, is the unsatisfactory performance unusual?

Answers to these questions should make it evident whether additional training could make a problem performer into a productive worker. Once you identify the need for training, then meet with the employee so you can together identify precisely what areas the individual is having problems with. (Some employees may have to be coaxed into admitting a training problem exists.)

In some instances staff members may be able to learn from each other; at other times you may want to arrange for formal training, either sending the individual(s) outside for training, bringing in-house a person to deliver the training, or providing the training yourself.

7. Structure Your Work Groups to Promote Learning

It is possible to set up work relationships so that members of the staff train each other. Using staff members with the needed skill to train those without it is less costly than either hiring a professional trainer or sending trainees outside to learn.

Here are three ways you can encourage your staff members to train each other:

1. *Networks.* This most often applies to use of new technology. In offices, often software users' networks are formed in which one member instructs the others or individual members share what they know with the rest of the group. But some trade associations also have networks that allow those within that discipline to get together and share information on the latest developments in their field. A high-value manager encourages staff members to join trade association networks to stay abreast of developments in their discipline as well as undergo organizational training to stay current with their company's procedures and practices.

2. *The buddy system.* The buddy system has one employee training another. Often a new hire is assigned to a seasoned pro to learn to do the job. This frees the manager from having to devote time to training the new hire. And it can be effective if the person chosen to buddy the recruit is able to train effectively in addition to do the job well. Remember, it takes tremendous patience to train another person. Further, as we all have

experienced at some point in our careers, some people are experts in their field but unable to share that expertise with others.

3. *Pair and share.* You are probably well aware that coworkers learn from one another and that benefits of teamwork are multiple. But it is more common for coworkers to form premanent teams than to routinely mix up the pairing. When the same two people work together regularly, they often develop a pattern in which they each use their strengths to compensate for areas of weakness in their partners. While this can work very well, it is limiting as far as individual growth is concerned.

Changing teams and partners can force employees to strengthen and then eliminate their areas of weakness if they are no longer paired with someone who will do those tasks for them. Instead of having two employees who can each do half a job, your goal should be to have two employees who can each do whatever is needed to get the job done.

8. Monitor On-the-Job Training

As we mentioned, there is much that can be learned from a good employee mistake, provided you don't swoop down on the person who made the mistake and fix it up in the name of damage control. Rather, you should discuss together what caused the problem and decide what should have been done differently. Yes, it's important to fix a problem that now exists, but don't be so quick to clean up the mess that the lesson is lost. Try to get the employee to identify for himself or herself where the error occurred, even if you have to drop some broad hints. Remember, a conclusion a person reaches by himself stays with him much longer than something that is merely told to him.

The Importance of Monitoring OTJ Training

Sometimes the person learning from a mistake is the manager rather than the employee. Consider our friend Carol, who heads up customer service. Her company had undergone some layoffs about six months before. Then, after three very tough months, the company did an economic turnaround that allowed Carol to hire three customer service reps. Although she was still short staffed in comparison to the prelayoff period, she felt her department was well positioned to handle customer queries for the firm's new products as well as its existing line. But instead service problems began to surface.

The company continuously surveyed customers. Until now, results had been better than good, but now the ratings were declining dramatically. Customers complained about being disconnected while on the line. Some interested in the new product line said they were transferred to product areas where the phone rang and rang. Still others felt they were rushed through their queries.

Carol didn't discover what the problem was until she spent a few minutes observing her rep team in action. It became evident to her that the problem lay not with one rep, but with six: the three new reps plus three long-timers. When a customer asked about the new product line, each immediately referred them to the product area, contrary to service policy. When too many calls were coming through at one time, the reps became short with the callers, cutting them off with a quick response, then slamming the phone down.

Carol decided to question Jed, one of the new reps. Jed had come from a firm with a glowing service record. She asked him what he thought about the quality of service he was providing his new company's clients, and Jed said, "It stinks, but then if it's all right with you, I guess it's all right with me."

Carol was startled. It wasn't all right with her, and never had been. She had trained her reps before, when she had had the time, but as her managerial job became busier and busier she had delegated the task to one of the reps on staff. Darlene was the latest person responsible for providing new hires with directions. While Darlene wasn't her best rep, she was longest with the firm, knew the company's product line backwards and forwards, and was highly skilled at using both the firm's database and phone system.

Jed told Carol that he was following instructions from Darlene. He felt he should answer product queries himself, but Darlene had said she often didn't have the time to do that during busy periods so she just referred it to the product group, which, after all, was better equipped than she to answer technical questions. Time spent on a call was monitored so she had told Jed and the other reps that it was best to move callers along as quickly as possible. She even confided that she occasionally hung up in the midst of a call to keep her record within standard. And the other reps were doing the same.

Carol was appalled. While Darlene was guilty of mislead-

ing the group, Carol had to blame [herself] for the situation.
She had not monitored the content of Darlene's instructions,
or even Darlene's own sloppy work habits, which were setting
a bad example for both the new reps and the old.

We share the story with you because it spotlights the importance of
monitoring the informal on-the-job training that occurs in a plant or office. Darlene hadn't been assigned to train the group, just asked by Carol
to answer questions the new hires might have. Yet the group's ability to
observe Darlene's bad work habits and receive her "good advice," was
sufficient to destroy a service rating that Carol had spent years developing.
        Think of your own office. To what extent does this kind of on-the-job
learning occur? It doesn't have to involve a new hire. A long-term employee asks a question and is given advice by another staffer who has
found a shortcut that works but is contrary to corporate policy because it
affects either the quality of the final product or service or is unsafe. The
person who asked the question uses the shortcut, then later shares it with
another staffer. After a while, a lot of bad work habits are being practiced
unbeknownst to the manager in charge.
        To prevent such a situation from happening:

■ *Monitor the performance of someone you ask to assist new hires before
you make the assignment.* Be sure that this person is doing the job right
before you make him or her responsible for training another employee.

■ *Explain the reasons why work is done the way it is, as well as how it
should be done.* Employees must be made to understand that procedures
that seem to waste time may actually ensure better product quality or
service, not to mention product safety or employee safety.

■ *Listen to employee ideas about how workflow can be improved.* If the idea
will increase productivity or reduce cost, implement it. If it won't, then
explain why you can't use the suggestion. High-value managers let their
staff know that they want to know about better ways of getting the work
done. Listening with an open mind to these ideas can increase productivity or decrease operating costs. But from a quality, service, or safety viewpoint, it also prevents problems from occurring by nipping ill-conceived
employee shortcuts in the bud.

■ *Set aside from thirty minutes a week to thirty minutes a day for employees
to learn new skills.* You act as trainer and take the staff through the new
practice of procedure.

- *Provide a central notebook or network database for employees to share ideas.* You can check the book or monitor the network to be sure that the right shortcuts and procedural suggestions are being exchanged.

- *Sponsor informal gatherings over lunch to share new information on learning.* Include not just full-time workers but part-time, flextime, and interns and temps in these sessions.

- *Create job aids for complex jobs or infrequent tasks.* This ensures that the job is done as it should be done. Some trainers believe that unmonitored, informal on-the-job learning—in which one employee asks another how to do a job and the other employee shows the individual the "wrong" way—may be responsible for quality or service problems that continue to exist regardless of the procedures and practices companies mandate.

9. Practice Action Learning

One way that high-value managers develop a learning environment is to practice action learning; that is, they use a real-world problem to help their staff develop new skills. Working on the problem replaces classroom instruction; the real-world problem is the equivalent of a case problem that M.B.A.s work on.

For instance, a group is formed to solve a costly operational problem. Before the team can get to work, it undergoes training in team-building skills, from brainstorming to reaching consensus. The team is likely taught these skills after it is formed. But as the team works on the problem, individual members' expertise in the skills taught grows from practice of the skills.

As the team works to solve the problem, under the direction of the team leader, who may or may not be their supervisor, they also develop more effective problem-solving and decision-making skills than they might have. We go into this in greater detail in Chapter 12, but know that the team leader, in his or her role as coach, can help the team perfect its problem-sensing and solving skills and consensus building. This is action learning at its best in that two results come from the effort: a successful idea and better-skilled staff members.

10. Take on the Teaching Role

High-value managers can send individual members to training courses or contract to have their entire staff trained at one time by an expert trainer. But they increasingly are doing the training themselves.

Here's how to prepare yourself to run an in-house training session:

- *Clarify the purpose of the training.* Your staff members have to understand the goal of the training they are being given. Tell them not only what you will be teaching but the purpose of the training: Why do they need to know what you are going to teach them?

- *Make learning groups manageable.* Will this training session be all lecture, or will it require hands-on particiation? Divide your department into groups according to what is most appropriate. In most cases, you will want to keep groups that are learning a hands-on skill small enough so that each member of the group can be given individual attention. A lecture class can be much larger. Discussion groups can range in size but should generally be kept small enough so that eye contact can be shared by all, all members can get a chance to speak, and group members are not intimidated by having to speak to a large group.

- *Prepare a lesson plan.* Knowing how to do something and knowing how to teach it are two different things. Prepare a lesson plan that will first identify what you need to teach about the subject and then how to best explain what you want trainees to learn. A lesson plan will prevent you from straying from the topic and will also help you cover the subject in its entirety.

- *Teach new procedures sequentially.* Demonstrate new techniques in the order in which they should be done. Don't skip one part and go back to it later; take your trainees through the process step by step.

- *Stop for questions.* Don't ask trainees to hold questions until the end. They may forget their questions at that time and then, when faced with doing the task on their own, may be unable to complete it. Answering questions as they come up will probably help to clarify issues for everyone.

- *Periodically test for comprehension.* You've prepared a lesson, thought it all out well, and delivered the lecture smoothly and succinctly. Unfortunately, unless you insist on getting feedback from the group, you'll have no way of knowing whether you succeeded in teaching anything until it is too late. Keep the session interactive even if it's a lecture. Ask questions and test employee comprehension of new concepts with hypothetical cases.

- *Hold a follow-up session.* Especially when teaching a new procedure, it is important to return to the group after it has had a chance to use its new knowledge. New questions will arise as staffers put the methods you've taught them into practice. By holding a follow-up meeting with the entire group, you enable members to share what they've learned and help one another solve any practical problems they may have encountered.

Don't limit your training to skill areas. As you empower your staff members and practice shared leadership, begin to grow the kinds of skills that will allow your staff to play a key role in the strategic leadership of your organization. This demands that you do much more than talk about your department's mission or vision. What that is will be discussed in the next chapter.

5

Making the Corporate Vision and Values a Reality

In Chapter 3, we told how important it is for you to communicate the goals and vision of your organization so that each employee can incorporate them into his or her daily actions. But to do this, realize that you need to do more than hold a stand-up or sit-down meeting at which you read a list of five to six values or a set of corporate goals to your staff members. High-value managers realize that support of the corporate mission, goals, and values begins during the planning process in which action plans are developed that specifically direct employee efforts toward these goals and values. Continued effort toward achieving the strategic direction of the organization is encouraged by recognition of staff efforts that support that focus and by the high-value manager's own example and words. Their actions support those of senior management and they see that the actions of staff members likewise support senior management's chosen direction and strategic intent.

It's important that employees can identify with the corporate vision and model their behavior accordingly. Two of the undisputed greats in this field, Sam Walton (Wal-Mart) and Bill Marriott (Marriott Corp.), were CEOs who embodied the credos they expected each of their employees to follow. Both men made frequent personal contact with employees at every level of their corporations and also with their customers. They not only preached the importance of good value and customer service, but they demonstrated it as well.

The successes of Sam Walton and Bill Marriott clarify the importance of spreading the word of the company's vision and goals and incorporating it into your employees' own goals and behavior on the job. In the planning process, ensuring that goals set reflect corporate direction is one of the best ways to link employee actions to organization philosophy and focus.

In this chapter we will discuss how, as a high-value manager, you will:

11. Hold goal-setting sessions.

12. Develop action plans that support the goals of the organization and corporate mission. With staff members, you set goals that are compatible with organizational objectives.

13. Prepare contingency plans that ensure that department goals, and therefore corporate objectives, are achieved.

14. Make departmental and corporate goals come alive for staff members by identifying the enablers that will allow the group to contribute to the corporate mission and goals. These enablers may take the form of resources or they may take the form of skills or abilities—employee competencies—critical to mission and goal achievement.

15. Maintain enthusiasm for action plans and objectives. Since these are so closely tied to corporate vision, the high-value manager also models the values the organization wishes to have practiced, whether they are value-added service or integrity and workplace diversity. For instance, you must demonstrate that you see people as individuals and value their contributions to the work unit regardless of their background or lifestyle.

11. Hold Goal-Setting Sessions

To prepare for a planning or goal-setting session, the high-value manager must:

- Be clear on management's planned direction for the organization. Understand the corporate vision and be prepared to explain it to your employees.
- Define your department's role in your organization. Identify what your department has traditionally been doing and also any possible expanded role for the department, as envisioned by you and top management.
- Make an outline of all points you want to cover during the meeting. While your ideas may be revised by the input of others during the meeting, you need to go into the goal-setting or planning meeting with a clear vision of how the group will support senior management's objectives and the corporate mission.
- Have a large writing board on which you can list suggestions from

> your employees. (Be prepared to list all the ideas that the group suggests, then pare them down to four or five objectives or goals for the year.)

- Prepare your employees before the meeting by asking them to think about the present and future goals of the department and to be ready to discuss them at the meeting.

12. Develop Goal-Supporting Action Plans

At the meeting itself, explain management's corporate vision, values, and goals. Often the highly coveted manager will spend the first hour or so of planning reviewing corporate objectives to help set the stage for the subsequent discussion of how the group can contribute to achievement of those goals. Once the group is clear about the corporate objectives or goals, it can write a mission statement that describes the department's mission in relationship to the organization's. Then the successful manager, together with his or her staff members, determines department objectives that will support the corporate objective and are in keeping with both the corporate and department mission.

Your employees are an excellent source for ideas. They know how to get their jobs done better than anyone. Make clear to them that you really want to hear what they have to say and are willing to change your thinking based on their arguments.

Generally, department goals are designed to increase the department's contribution to the bottom line by either reducing costs or increasing profits. But there may also be goals that are not directly linked to financials. For instance, the organization may have determined that it wants to be the enterprise with the best product quality record in its field. Or it might have determined that customer service will enable the firm to stand apart from its competitors. Or the thrust may be on new products or services for the current clients or greater client retention through consultative selling. Department or division objectives cascade from these broader objectives.

The best-written goals reflect the SMART model; that is, they are:

- *Specific.* They state specifically what will be accomplished.
- *Measurable.* They are quantifiable, either by cost savings or profit contribution.
- *Attainable.* They are achievable.

- *Realistic.* The work group believes it can achieve the objective it has set.
- *Time sensitive.* A date is set by which time the objective or goal is to be achieved.

As the group identifies the goals, the high-value manager or a facilitator writes these down on a flip chart. None should be evaluated until the group has finished its creative thinking. Then the manager may want to work with the group to choose three or four goals to pursue—or whatever number is realistic.

To make the choice, the group might begin by attempting to link some of the goals on the flip chart, reducing the number from which they choose those to focus their attention on. Goals will be defined according to their relationship to the corporate vision or mission, but it is equally important that the group consider the resources each goal will require and whether the organization can expend those resources—from dollars to people's time to the purchase of new equipment—to achieve the goal.

Once the group chooses those goals on which to focus its attention, it then develops action plans that will enable it to achieve each of its objectives. It may empower a member of the group to research an area with potential for greater profitability or move ahead to produce a new product or service or cut costs. If more than one person may be involved in achieving the goal, the group might develop a flow chart, with schedule and specific assignments for each staff member. The flow chart diagrams each of the actions to be taken and the sequence in which it must occur. Names of specific staff member are placed beside each task in the flow chart.

Some action plans are best developed by forward scheduling, that is, planning moves from start-up to completion date. Backward scheduling begins with a completion date, and the work group works out how it will finish the project, and achieve its objective, by that time.

Afterwards, while writing up the goal-setting session, the high-value manager should evaluate the final plans. To help in this review, he or she should ask:

- Does the plan contribute to the achievement of the department goal and, therefore, the corporate goals?
- Are the underlying assumptions valid?
- Is it clear what is to be done and why?
- Is it clear who will be responsible for the tasks that make up the plan?

- Is the plan feasible? If it isn't, how can it be made feasible?
- How can the plan's progress be monitored to determine if it is succeeding?
- Is the cost of implementation higher than payback?
- How will we measure the plan's success?

13. Prepare Contingency Plans

If this review suggests there may be some weakness in the plan, then it may be appropriate to spend some further time revising it.

Even then, despite our best efforts, action plans may not succeed. Groups sometimes make assumptions that are unlikely to be true. Or they try to plan too far ahead. Or unforeseen events occur either within or outside the organization, beyond the staff members' control. Plans may also depend for realization on the efforts of others, who may not be motivated to help, or on the commitment of time, people, or other resources that senior management proves to be unable to make. Many companies flow in and out of economic stability in this period of constant change and cannot always follow through with promises of financial support.

For whatever reason, some of the plans made during the planning or goal-setting meeting may not work.

Perhaps the problem isn't identified during this review. But later problems arise. A high-value manager includes controls within each action plan to monitor progress and consequently is able to react quickly should problems arise with the original plan. This quick response is important. Too often people wait too long to adjust or change an action plan and consequently fail to achieve the group objective or goal.

Since the goal may be directly tied to corporate goals, even the corporate bottom line, quick-response management is critical.

Understand that the high-value manager doesn't walk away from either the goal or action plan if the plan is not working. Generally during goal setting, some time is spent identifying the factors critical to the action plan and estimating how they would go awry. Actions are taken then to prevent these problems from happening. But when problems still occur, then the group comes together to develop a contingency plan (a Plan B) that will enable the group still to achieve its objective. The group rethinks how it is to achieve the planned outcome. New avenues are identified, and a new schedule is determined to achieve the goal.

Sometimes, a review of the situation suggests that the goal at this point can't be reached. Modification of the plan or even the goal isn't sufficient. Or a new plan may negatively affect an existing plan, drawing vital resources from it, and the new goals and objectives have to be adjusted. Or one department's objective overlaps or conflicts with another's. Then the high-value manager has to make tough decisions about available resources and areas of responsibility.

When Departmental Goals Conflict

Hal, warehouse manager, and his friend Tim, who heads up shipping, found themselves with conflicting goals during one of their regular lunches together. Both had gone through goal-setting sessions with their work groups, and they had both identified ways to get product to their customers faster—a major objective of the organization, tied to its value of improved customer service. But when the two revealed their departmental plans over lunch, it became clear that implementing Hal's idea in the warehouse would slow up Tim's shipping operation. And if Tim's plans to speed up shipping were implemented, warehousing would have problems controlling inventory.

The two managers laughed when they realized that neither had taken the other's workflow into consideration during planning. Putting their heads together, they soon concluded that both ideas were still possible with some major changes in the way work was done.

Their two groups could contribute to the organization's strategic goal of improved customer service, but it would take more planning. Hal and Tim also agreed that in the future they would include the other in any group planning sessions.

The moral: Goal setting has to take the total organization into consideration. Which means not only how goals can impede another area's operation but also how goals set by one department can help another's, thereby indirectly contributing to the corporate mission. Or how one group can help another group to achieve its plan. (See Section IV, Teams and Team Management.)

14. Identify the Enablers

The high-value manager recognizes that time, materials, people, knowledge, and equipment may all be needed to make a plan succeed. Ideas are a dime a dozen; implementation is the tough part of any planning, and implementation requires a clear idea of the resources needed.

The most important question that the high-value manager will ask himself is: Is the group goal and plan worth it? What will it contribute to the bottom line? This, too, needs to be addressed by the group during the goal-setting or planning meeting. We tend to think of resources as dollars or equipment or raw materials. But recognize that a part of any cost-benefit analysis has to be the staff time committed to the effort. A high-value manager looks at the full picture, which might show that equipment and raw materials are readily available and within cost parameters but staff time makes the plan too costly. Adding people might be impossible, and existing staff may not have the time to support the effort.

There may be ways around these resource problems, and the group will work to identify them. But do know that some ideas may have to be thrown out, or at least delayed, if the analysis suggests that the costs are too high for implementation.

The abilities of staff to accomplish the goals and action plan are other enablers that need to be considered. We read daily about the new applications of ever-changing technology. These represent wonderful competitive opportunities for companies, provided their staff is able to use the new technology. Part of the plan might have to include training for one or all staff members, and that needs to be considered as the group meets in goal setting.

Remember, all goals must support senior management's objectives and the corporate vision and mission, but they also must conform with the SMART model, which means that they must be attainable and realistic.

15. Maintain Enthusiasm

Throughout implementation of the action plan, the high-value manager meets with those responsible for parts of the project, not only to determine the project's status but to communicate how important the plan is to the support of the group's goal and, in turn, support of a corporate goal or value. Monthly meetings might be held with the entire group to get progress reports, thereby building group interest in the work under way, plus involving employees in the process as much as possible.

The successful manager makes himself or herself available to those involved in achieving plans to address any problems encountered in working on the project. If a staff member needs a hand, the high-value manager may roll up his or her sleeves to assist or redelegate work within the department to ensure that the staff member has the time to commit to the plan. If it appears that allocations about staff time were unrealistic, then the high-value manager may have to reconvene the goal-setting group to reconsider its action plan, maybe even reconsider the goal.

The high-value manager undertakes planning with the corporate objectives clearly in mind. He or she is familiar with the organization as a whole and shares this knowledge in the goal-setting process and with individual staff members to enable them to achieve the plans that will support the organization.

We've been talking about hard plans and vision to date, as well as values like value-added quality and customer service. But do know that the manager is as responsible for supporting the softer values of the organization. The organization may have strong ethical beliefs and value diversity, for example, and it is the high-value manager's responsibility to promote these, along with more bottom-line values to staff. We know of a manager who chose to pay out money that delayed early profit on a product to provide a better-quality product to his customer. The message sent was one about customer service. But it also said something about the manager's integrity. Staff members had suggested that the product be sent, as is, with some shortcomings, then the next batch changed to include the improvements. This high-value manager nicked the idea, preferring a more ethical approach with the customer.

That sent a strong message to his work group about what he valued—good service and ethical behavior.

6

Staying Current and Flexible

In today's workplace, where change is the norm, not the exception, the highly coveted manager is one who is adaptable, flexible enough to accept not only the new supervisory style that we have discussed in earlier chapters but also new work relationships and new ways to get the work done. As a high-value manager, you stay abreast of developments in technology and people management and work smart by applying these to your workplace if they will either increase productivity or reduce operating costs. You:

16. Deemphasize job titles in order to build the kind of cooperative work environment that has proven to be most productive.

17. Effectively use part-time employees, job-sharing, contracted services, temps, and interns to cope with uneven workflow or tight staff budgets.

18. Offer telecommuting options to full-time staff to increase motivation and/or reduce the need for office space.

19. Lead others in using the new technology. The high-value manager is someone others look to for information about the new technology because he or she is up on the latest developments.

20. Use the new technology—rather than the tried and true—only where it represents a solid business solution. Still, the new technology might solve a problem yet to be encountered, and the successful manager takes that longer-term view, as well as costs, into consideration in making the tough buying decisions in the present. In making decisions about introducing new technology in the office or plant, you understand that the use of new technology involves a learning curve and include that in any plans or projections you develop to bring in the new technology.

16. Deemphasize Job Titles

The use of the word "associate" for rank and file is more than a matter of semantics. It reflects the change in the way companies operate. In today's organizations, people from rank and file are colleagues—"associates"— coming together to achieve their organization's objectives. When staff are treated as associates, as well as called associates, they give to the organization the very best effort they can.

Highly coveted managers recognize the high performance that can come from the deemphasis on job titles. They realize that individuals bring to their jobs unique skills, talents, and experiences not necessarily reflected in job titles. Title is a yardstick, but it is only one yardstick among many.

In the past, job titles were cherished by their holders. It mattered whether one was an assistant or an associate whatever, a junior or a senior something or other. No more. The traditionally managed workplace of the past in which job titles were so prized has been replaced by the newer, more dynamic organization of the present in which people no longer operate in little boxes like those found on organization charts. Studies suggest that staff members prefer these boundaryless organizations because they offer training and development opportunities and challenges that otherwise might not have been available. Getting to the bottom line, they are motivated to produce more.

To refuse to adapt to the new verbiage is as detrimental to the organization's health as failing to utilize the skills of a talented staff member to solve a major problem because his or her job description doesn't include that task. Which is what refusing to deemphasize title could lead to, as high-value managers recognize. These managers' outlook allows them to see the benefits—to their organization, their staff members, and themselves—of treating staff as associates. Managers, or "coaches," thereby need to devote less time to performance improvement; the associates monitor themselves and each other.

17. Implement New Work Relationships

While today's organizations offer more opportunity to explore one's abilities, they are also leaner than in the past, with no staff fat to accommodate last-minute assignments and seasonal shifts toward higher output and to fill staffing holes created by turnover or vacation schedules. Which is why our high-value managers welcome the increase in professionalism of con-

tracted services individuals, the availability of temps in areas besides cler-
ical support, the desire on the part of high school and college students to
be temps to learn about the business world, and the growing numbers
of individuals interested in part-time work. When well supervised, these
individuals can do more than just fill the gaps; they can contribute significantly to the organization's competitive advantage.

One word of warning: Before pursuing any of these arrangements,
check with Human Resources to identify any legal issues to be complied
with. For instance, the IRS has set certain guidelines to differentiate full-
time staff members from those on contract. Failure to make a clear distinc-
tion can cost your company considerable overtime and benefits costs.
Likewise, be sure that your temp's agency provides workers' compensa-
tion coverage. Otherwise, your firm might be held liable should an acci-
dent occur that disables the employee. Temps, those on contract, interns,
and part-timers are covered by the same legislation that protects full-time
staff, from antidiscrimination legislation to harassment.

To understand how to make the most of one of these work relationships, consider the case of Janie:

The Temp Who Cares

Janie, an accountant, is a temp reporting to Priscilla, chief financial officer at her company. When Priscilla's organization
downsized several months ago, she lost two staff members.
The company is slowly stabilizing economically, but in this
period of transition Priscilla could not get approval to hire a
staff accountant to handle the increased workload that came
from the acquisition of a new division by the company. So
Priscilla chose to go to a temporary agency that supplied ac-
countants.

Before choosing the agency, she wisely checked with colleagues in the field to identify the best firm available. She also
spent considerable time with the agency's recruiter to be sure
that the temp who came would have the skills and experience
Priscilla needed.

Besides trying to fill her staffing needs with the best by
going to a reputable agency and seeing that the agency was
well aware of her needs, Priscilla, who has more than once
proven her worth to her firm, recognized the importance of
treating Janie with the same respect as a permanent staff member. That respect was shown from day one when Priscilla spent

about two hours with Janie explaining the department's role, describing the new division and Janie's responsibilities in it, and introducing the people with whom Janie would be working.

There are four full-time staff members besides Priscilla, and once a month Priscilla and her staff (which, of course, includes Janie) meet to review progress during the previous month over a lunch of sandwiches and sodas in Priscilla's office. Janie has been made to feel like a member of the team, and she more than carries her weight. Recently in reviewing some bills she recognized a scam being played on the new division's purchasing department. Invoices were sent and approved by harried managers who had not looked carefully to be sure that the supplies invoiced had ever been ordered, let alone been received. Janie was able to catch the ploy because she had seen a similar scam some years before while working as a full-time staff member at another company. The savings to the company were in the tens of thousands of dollars.

At Priscilla's request, Janie received the company's distinguished service award. This award is normally given to full-time staff members, but Janie received it because, as the note written by Priscilla accompanying the prize said, "Janie gave the company the attention it would get if she were a full-time staff member. She had earned the recognition."

If Janie had not been made to feel important to the team, she might not have been as conscientious in reviewing accounts payable as they came over her desk, and might not have identified the false paperwork. But Priscilla had created a work environment of which Janie could feel a real part. Priscilla's formula is one that all managers should follow given the return in invested time. Priscilla:

▪ Listened to Janie's ideas. Because temps usually have worked for several companies, they often have insights into how the work can be done better. Even interns, while new to the job market, may raise questions during the first few days on the job that can make you rethink how your department works. You might ask, "Why didn't I think of that?" Or, "Why *have* we been doing this?"

▪ Included Janie in project meetings. When Priscilla needed a member of her staff to participate in a project to develop new accounts receivable guidelines, she chose Janie. This sent a message to Janie and her coworkers about the respect for Janie. Soon Priscilla's staffers, too, were seeking Janie out for help. Janie also was learning from the staff, so both she and the staffers grew professionally from the exchange.

- Reviewed Janie's performance and shared her conclusions with Janie. Most managers give feedback to the temp agency rather than the temp. Priscilla recognized that the real payoff for such evaluations came from sharing them with the temp. Certainly Janie appreciated Priscilla's interest in her professional development, and it further motivated her.

- Invested in Janie's development. When two of Priscilla's staffers attended a single-day program sponsored by an accounting consultancy, Priscilla had Janie go along. Even though she paid for the time spent, Priscilla felt she was gaining in the long term by having a better-skilled staffer.

- Kept Janie informed about developments that had nothing to do with Janie's own work. Not only did this allow Janie to easily step in to help other staffers who might be absent, but once again it sent a message to Janie and the staff that Janie was important to the group.

In short, Priscilla treated Janie in the same ways she treated her own staff—and not only professionally. She saw that Janie was invited to luncheons to celebrate team member birthdays and other happy occasions, even on days in which Janie wasn't expected in the office. Priscilla realized it wasn't so important whether Janie showed up or not—although she hoped that she would choose to come during her own time—but that she knew that everyone wanted her to come, no matter what the day of the week.

The rules above apply, whether the individual is a temp, intern, contracted services person, or part-timer. They are designed to maximize the benefits from the working relationship with someone who isn't on staff permanently or full-time.

Flextime is another work relationship that demands managers are adaptable, as was Rose's boss in the following case study.

A Flextime Success Story

Rose has a small child, Max, for whom she hires a caregiver to come to her home. The caregiver, Esther (who lives nearby), must see her own children off to school before she can leave to be with Max. School schedules' being inflexible, this means that Esther cannot be at Rose's home until eight–forty-five. Rose can usually be out the door by nine, but she commutes to the city from the suburbs and so will not arrive at work much before ten.

As is traditional, Rose's workplace opens for business at nine. Before Max was born, Rose was always in on time, but Max's presence has complicated things. If arriving by nine is a necessity, Rose has a limited range of options. She can:

1. *Find a caregiver who will be able to arrive earlier.* This option must be ruled out because Rose feels that Esther gives Max the best, most loving care possible. She doubts that anyone else would be as satisfactory as Esther and therefore refuses to compromise her son's well-being to make this change.
2. *Quit her job.* The catch here is that Rose likes her job and needs the income from it to support herself and her family.
3. *Request that her hours be changed so that she comes in later and works later.* This tentative solution would work best for Rose—but it requires the cooperation of Rose's manager. If you were that manager, what would you do?

Here's what Rose's manager did: Appreciating her value as an employee, he decided to make the accommodation to keep her. He even opened the door to flextime for the rest of the staff. His only proviso: There had to be sufficient people on staff at nine to be available to handle client phone calls and visits, and staff members had to keep each other sufficiently acquainted with the accounts on which they worked and record-keeping systems so that customer service did not decline to accommodate the staff's personal needs.

The staff was more than willing to meet weekly to review progress on each client's work to be sure to keep service quality at a level to allow those who wanted flextime to have it. Some members liked Rose's schedule, others preferred to arrive early and leave early, and there were some staff members who were content with the nine-to-five system. The weekly get-togethers helped staffers to field others' phone calls during lunch hours and prepared them to answer customer queries. The new arrangement worked well for the staff and manager, so everyone was satisfied.

18. Allow Telecommuting

While Rose was able to accommodate her personal problem by arriving and leaving later in the day, some staff members need a full day off to deal with a problem. When the problem is connected with their home—perhaps some repair work in the kitchen or delivery of an important piece of furniture—they may ask to work at home rather than take the day off as a vacation day. If an employee with a track record of reliability makes such a request, high-value managers say yes, assuming there is no corporate policy against it, since a satisfied worker is a highly productive one. Some staff members are well prepared to work at home, having home offices with as much, if not more, office equipment than their company office has. Where the work allows and employees have proven to be reliable, some managers have even set policies that allow each employee x days (usually one day) per month to work at home if personal circumstances require it.

For those employees with long commutes, on bad weather days, this can be a blessing. For the company, there is also the benefit of greater worker productivity, since an employee trapped in traffic tied up by a snowstorm or icy roads isn't very worthwhile to the company. So long as the work is done, and high-value managers put into place control techniques that allow them to monitor work-at-home days, the policy works for everyone.

But the greater accessibility of office technology is prompting increasing numbers of employees to ask to be allowed to work at home on a regular basis. *Computerworld* recently reported that 7.6 million Americans work away from their offices. The trend is growing as companies see noticeable increases in productivity and worker satisfaction and decreases in overhead costs. In fact, full departments now telecommute, linked together by phone, computers, and fax, with an occasional in-person meeting to tie down loose ends.

This shift in the way work is done demands tremendous flexibility on the part of managers. Highly coveted ones, who have learned to bend rather than snap when buffeted by the winds of change, allow telecommuting when the benefits to the employee(s) and organization outweigh the costs in dollars or lost productivity. This is determined by three factors:

1. *Does the work lend itself to telecommuting?* Those jobs best suited to telecommuting are ones in which the employee works alone, like writing, editing, data manipulation, sales, and telemarketing. If all the staff member needs is a desk, a computer, and a phone, with occasional contact with office staff, then telecommuting may be a viable alternative work arrangement.

2. *Can the work be monitored?* There need to be controls to be sure that the work is done while an employee is at home. Not everyone can concentrate on work while at home given the many distractions there—from a demanding child to television to personal errands. In the case of an individual request to work at home, high-value managers take into consideration the track record of the individual making the request. Can the manager rely on the employee to work at home as promised? If the entire department is being considered for telecommuting, are there any staff members who should be transferred elsewhere, where work is still done in the office?

3. *How much will telecommuting cost the organization?* Of the three questions, this may be the most pivotal, influencing the final decision about either one or many employees being able to telecommute.

If a staffer has his or her own computer, that's a start. But full-time telecommuting in some jobs may demand having almost a complete workstation at home, something that most employees can't afford to set up themselves. Consequently, the company might have to install a dedicated telephone line, purchase and install fax and copier equipment, and modemize the computer, linking it to the office. Multiply this cost by the number of employees who might demand the right to telecommute after one of their colleagues is given approval to do so and the costs could far outweigh the benefits in increased performance that comes from greater employee satisfaction. Needless to say, allowing a full department to work at home may sound good in television ads in which a boss announces to his staff that from now on they can all work at home if they choose, given the latest technology, but technological capability isn't the only issue—and high-value managers recognize that. Costs of effective telecommuting must be measured against decreased ovehead costs.

High-value managers see telecommuting not as a benefit but as a solution to a business problem: that problem is the growing cost of office space combined with the difficulty in finding highly qualified staff who are affordable on a full-time basis. Where telecommuting is a cost-effective solution, then it is a viable option, and successful managers adapt their office situation to it, from providing the technology to the telecommuter to holding monthly staff briefings to see that the telecommuter stays in touch with his or her "coworkers," to assigning the telecommuter an in-house buddy who is kept informed daily of the telecommuter's activities so nothing falls between the cracks.

19. Lead Others in Using the New Technology

In talking about the adaptability of high-value managers, we would be remiss if we didn't mention his or her flexibility in accepting the new technology. Ideally, all companies should be at the forefront of technology—whether we're talking about CAD, CAM, MRPII, or Internet and the information superhighway. But not all companies have reached this stage, given budgetary constraints. But the high-value manager stays abreast of developments to be prepared to implement technology within the organization's means that will address specific business problems while he or she works with the technology his or her company currently can afford. The high-value manager's knowledge makes him or her a leader to whom other managers look for answers about their technical needs.

How has the high-value manager become so knowledgeable? Just using the high-value manager in the office setting as an example, he or she is a regular reader of the various computer magazines being written for nontechies that rate everything from hardware to software, to modems, to printers, and that outline these equipments' applicability. Highly coveted managers also visit other business sites and examine how these companies use the new technology. They attend trade shows and exhibits in which the new technology they might need to use is explored.

Knowledgeable about what best works where, the successful manager is able to make a strong case for that technology that could reduce operating costs while increasing productivity, although there is a short-term dollars outlay. Comparisons of his or her operation to that within another organization—"benchmarking"—identifies opportunities for increased efficiencies, higher productivity, and reduced costs that can help sway senior management to loosen the purse strings, as well.

Consequently, high-value managers' departments or divisions are often the test sites for the systems department to try out the newest technology. And often these applications prove more than worthwhile. The highly coveted manager can describe the business problem in terms that the systems person can understand because the high-value manager has stayed abreast of technological developments.

20. Buy the Right Tools for the Right Tasks

We have noted how the high-value manager stays current with technological developments. But let us stress here that the successful manager uses judgment about the new techniques and tools that he or she reads about or studies. Not everything is appropriate for his application or business problem. He doesn't purchase something because it is the latest, the biggest, the best. Nor does he jump into every management program or fad; some will work for him, some won't, and the high-value manager makes judgments about which will be productive and which won't.

We're not just talking about the dollar costs of purchasing new equipment. There's a learning curve with every new program or effort that costs in terms of productivity. As employees learn new procedures or focus attention in new directions, their day-to-day productivity can be affected. So you have to be discriminating about which products or programs to pursue. The high-value manager knows this.

No question about it, it's a balancing act. You have to think about short-term needs but, as you solve problems in the near term, you have to be looking to the longer term as well. Even as you determine the solution to a current problem you have to be configuring how changes in that solution can be made to address future problems.

Let's look at technology as a case in point. If there are any rules to follow, it is these:

- *Conduct a needs assessment.* What does your department need now? What will it need in the future? Is there an advantage to making a more expensive purchase today to prepare for future needs?

- *Don't overpurchase.* Use judgment. Don't buy into the hoopla that comes with the new technology. Be realistic in your decisions about what you need.

- *Think long-term if you can afford it.* A LAN network is preferable to individual computers if you see greater flow of work among staff members as something that will happen in the future. Access to the information superhighway and Internet means immediate access to information that can make it easier to do your work, suggest new ideas for products, or identify a new market. If you can't modemize all your computers, begin with two or three to provide the wealth of information to your department. Develop an action plan that calls for all machines to be linked to Internet within five years.

- *Manage the learning curve.* Recognize that there will be some loss of productivity in the beginning, and plan for it. Involve systems personnel in the initial and ongoing training. Support an internal users' group whose members can help each other with current technology and to master the new technology. The high-value manager knows that change is constant, and he sets an example for the rest of the work team in responding to change. We mentioned how the winds of change are buffeting businesses. High-value managers don't fight change—they have seen trees snap in the wind. Rather, successful managers know how to make change work for their organizations.

Section III

A Commitment to Continuous Improvement

"If it ain't broke, don't fix it." High-value managers know otherwise. They realize that every area of an operation demands observation and analysis on a regular basis to determine if it can be done more efficiently or more effectively. They practice preventive management and teach their employees problem-solving and decision-making skills that enable them to make continuous improvements in their own areas as well.

They themselves are proactive when it comes to solving problems, identifying areas during planning where problems may arise, creating contingency plans, or B Plans, that overcome problems that might happen if. . . .

But they do more than that to bring about continuous improvement. They risk by entering the white spaces between defined responsibilities to achieve better bottom-line results. And they encourage their staff members to do likewise. They encourage and reward employee initiative, even when it creates some political explosions, if it contributes to the good of the organization.

In the area of quality and service, they are forever seeking new and better ways to satisfy customers, internal as well as external. They see their role in Michael Porter's value chain in achieving competitive advantage.

7

Practicing Preventive Management

Problem solving can take up a lot of managerial time. So it makes sense for you to resolve problems before they develop, let alone grow to impact the bottom line. As a high-value manager you practice preventive management for just this reason. You understand how problems often can be identified in their early stages, even avoided. You know how important it is to analyze an operation or practice to determine where weaknesses can occur and then shore up these weaknesses or, better yet, develop procedures without such flaws.

In short, as a high-value manager, you recognize that the best approach to problem solving is to avoid a serious problem in the first place. This isn't easy but it is possible. Early problem detection and better problem solving demand that you:

21. Create an environment in which employees are encouraged to use their initiative to remedy problems when they first occur. Risk is allowed. High-value managers aren't risk adverse.

22. Undertake problem sensing. The high-value manager leads staff members in using a variety of techniques to locate problems and then determine the root cause, not just a symptom of the problem. Too often a problem reappears because its symptoms, not the reason for them, have been the focus of attention.

23. View problems as opportunities and mistakes as progress. This involves turning traditional thinking about problems upside down. But with some creativity, problems can lead to opportunities; mistakes in problem solving can be progress toward achieving these opportunities. A high-value manager recognizes this and teaches creative thinking techniques to staff to stimulate their thinking outside the box.

24. Practice techniques that enable you to choose the best solution from several good ones.

25. Communicate solutions to the rest of the organization. The high-value manager shares what his or her group has discovered to save other groups within the company from having to reinvent the wheel. Such trail-blazing makes the high-value leader and his or her staff organizational heroes, but they communicate their discoveries because they are good corporate citizens and because the high-value manager knows everyone benefits from working in a profitable organization.

21. Encourage Initiative

The high-value manager gives truth to his or her talk of shared goals and leadership by allowing staff members to step out of their boxes and demonstrate in a supportive environment their personal creativity. After all, encouraging employee initiative makes sense. By allowing employees a more active role in problem solving, the high-value manager increases staff members' feelings of satisfaction with their jobs while freeing himself or herself to devote attention to planning or other managerial tasks.

The foundations are laid for employees to resolve problems on their own when the high-value manager includes staff in goal setting and development of action plans. If staff members are to address on their own problems they find as they do their work, they need that information. It helps them to make the right decisions and focus their energies where it will have the greatest return for the organization. But tapping into mission or goals isn't always sufficient. Nor do bromides about the value of employee initiative constitute a supportive environment for out-of-the-box thinking for staff members.

Squelching Initiative: Sallie's Case

Sallie is head of marketing for a farm equipment manufacturer we'll call Farmeq. In principle, she believes in empowering employees to make decisions and solve problems related to their own work. She practices it by including her staff in goal setting and planning, but nothing more. Sallie often complains about the frequency with which sales personnel call with problems for her to solve, unaware that her actions often belie her words about employees' solving their own work problems. Recently at a staff meeting, she demonstrated how little she truly believes in encouraging employee initiative by tearing into one of her staff members who had taken her up on her offer to think out of the box.

On his own, Joe, who was relatively new in the organization, had met with and negotiated a deal with a firm to market some of Farmeq's products overseas at the same time it marketed its own. Unbeknownst to Joe, but known to Sallie, Farmeq had already committed itself to a partnership with a major corporation. It wasn't an industry secret. It was just that Sallie never thought to share the information with her staff. But Joe had several foreign subsidiaries in his sales area, and they had told him that orders for product were handled by their overseas headquarters. Joe felt that it would be a coup if he could land some of these major firms' business. Consequently, his plan of action and the subsequent legal hassle almost enveloped Farmeq in.

Sallie lost her cool—and the respect of her sales staff—when she came down on Joe for doing exactly what she has espoused—taking initiative. After all, as the sales force thought, she had helped create the situation herself by not keeping the group informed about the planned partnership. Will Joe use his initiative again? Unlikely. Sallie's reaction to his mistake was so dramatic that it likely discouraged him and his peers from ever again taking upon themselves the initiative to solve a problem. Sallie will find her workday busier than ever answering her sales force's questions.

Yes, there is a risk associated with granting employees the freedom to take initiative. But high-value managers aren't risk adverse. They recognize that increasing an employee's freedom over his or her work may have costly and tumultuous repercussions, but they recognize, too, that they will benefit from having on staff employees who may be more productive and who may bring clearer insights to problems from their proximity to them. They are also wise enough to minimize the risks through training and placement of control systems that allow them to stay abreast of employee actions.

A high-value manager creates an environment in which encouraging employee initiative can be relatively safe. They do this by:

■ *Keeping all lines of communication open.* By holding bimonthly or monthly staff meetings in which members of the sales force shared their

plan and she updated them on headquarters or departmental developments, Sallie certainly could have avoided the problem with Joe. Make a
concerted effort to share information with your staff members—even if
you think they don't need that information to do their jobs. The more
your employees know about company events, deadlines, difficulties with
suppliers, and the like, the better equipped they are to make intelligent
decisions when problems arise.

   • *Listening.* Joe had been complaining for some time about the location of so many foreign subsidiaries in his territory. Sallie never really
heard his complaints. Consequently, she never met with him to develop
some specific action plans to help him make up for lost sales from his
region.

   If you worry that you may not have sufficient time to hear out all
ideas, in some instances you may want to have an employee check with
you before implementing a plan.

   • *Giving frequent, objective, and initiative-encouraging feedback.* Even
when a problem arises from their use of their initiative, you don't want
to dwell so much on that that you discourage further risk taking by the
employee. They need to be counseled on what specifically they did wrong
and what specifically they did right, and coached, in general, on solving
problems.

   • *Conducting ongoing training where it is evidently needed.* If an employee makes a mistake in solving a problem, and it is likely that that
problem might be encountered again, then you might want to have the
person undergo training in that part of the solution where he or she is
weak. Say you have someone who suddenly found himself required to
set terms with a representative for another firm for purchase of his firm's
services. The person did a bad negotiating job. So you might want to have
that individual undergo some training in negotiation for the next time
the problem crops up. Or suggest that there is a point in problem solving
where he needs to bring you into the negotiation; then he can observe and
learn from your negotiation style and determine what terms represent a
win/win situation for both firms.

   How do you get your staff members to bring solutions to you instead
of problems? Employees will sometimes resist having to make a decision
because they feel it is their manager's call. High-value managers realize
this and so intentionally pull back more than they are accustomed to do
to force their employees to come up with a solution.

   Getting employees who have never demonstrated initiative to do so can take several stages. When an employee first brings a problem to you, you might come up with the solution. The next time she brings the same problem or a related one, you might ask her for a suggestion. If she has none, you might remind her about what was done before and ask if that suggests something. Next time the person comes to you, you might suggest she go back and think about the problem and bring at least one solution to you. In coaching your employees in problem solving, encourage them to go beyond one or two tries at a solution. Allowing them to give up too soon will only make them hand the problem over to you instead of trying another solution.

If a person has successfully solved a number of problems dealing with a particular issue, make a big deal of it. Tell him or her, "I doubt you'll need much more help from me when something like this happens; I trust you to decide how to deal with the problem." If the person still brings problems after that, simply say, "I trust you to decide how to solve this problem. You've already handled this situation very well several times."

In time, the staff member may become so confident that he or she will proudly report on actions taken independently either at your staff meeting or in writing as a part of the report mechanism you have set up to control your efforts to increase employee initiative.

22. Undertake Problem Sensing

Although problem solving is a six-step process, know that most employees, whether independently or working in teams, want to move immediately to step 3 (identifying solutions), so a key role as supervisor or leader of a team will be to hold the person or group back until it has thoroughly studied the problem or situation. Problem sensing begins by defining the nature of the problem (step 1). That entails focusing on the "what," or cause of the problem, maybe even putting the cause in writing. Once you do that, you can move on to the gathering of information (step 2).

There are a number of techniques that can be used. Most problems leave paper trails, and careful analysis of printouts, marketing research findings, and other data can cast a light on a problem or suggest a new product idea that further research can confirm.

Insight from employees may also be worth gathering. Just as in marketing, in which groups of potential customers are often brought together to give feedback on a new product idea—focus groups—in problem solving you might want to hold focus groups with employees or those affected by a problem to get their ideas about the cause.

There are more sophisticated problem-sensing tools as well that you may want to bring to bear on the problem, like Pareto analysis, scatter diagrams, workflow diagrams, cause and effect diagrams, and variance analysis, that will help you separate symptoms from causes. Information on these techniques may be found in most textbooks about quality improvement since these techniques are often linked to that issue. However, here are some brief descriptions of these problem-sensing techniques:

- *Pareto Analysis.* This technique recognizes that many things may be happening that are creating problems but only a few of these may be key to the situation. Your intent should be to identify those critical few and address those in order to resolve the situation. Measurable data are necessary for such analysis, so the initial step may be to gather information on quality or cost or productivity. Then the data are analyzed to determine which elements are having the most impact—whether it is people being put on hold or warehousing problems that are creating customer service complaints or missed delivery dates. The process assumes that 20 percent of the factors impact 80 percent of the time; the next step, then, is to identify action plans to address those 20 percent of the elements. (See Figure 7-1.)

- *Scatter Diagrams.* These diagrams study the relationship between two factors—problem and situation—to see how often they occur at the same time. The more scattered the events and timelines of problems, the less likely the two factors are related to each other. You might compare a number of problem incidents to use of product from a supplier or a particular piece of equipment or even an employee on the line to identify the likelihood of cause of the problem incidents. (See Figure 7-2.)

- *Workflow Diagrams.* These show the flow of materials, people, or information within any organization. Detailed workflow charts will help to identify at what point in a process problems affect the system, usually because work has to be redone at that point. (See Figure 7-3.)

- *Cause and Effect Diagrams.* The team first carefully determines the nature of the problem. It then identifies likely causes of the problem, ultimately reaching agreement on the major causes. The members then try to visually connect all the causes back to the general problem, drawing lines to show relationships between causes and relationships. More lines are drawn as additional causes are traced to these problems. In searching for

Figure 7-1. Pareto analysis.

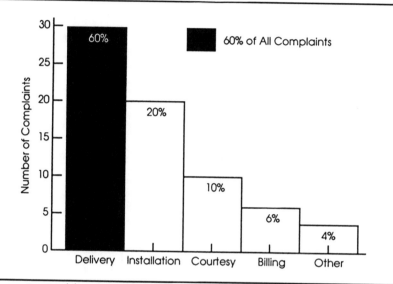

causes, the team ultimately comes to the root cause of the problem, the one they need to address before they can address the others.

Because the final diagram often resembles a fishbone, the technique is also called fishbone analysis. (See Figure 7-4.)

▪ *Variance Analysis.* All the steps necessary to produce a product or complete a process are studied to determine where problems are likely to occur and their consequences. Once you have identified likely causes, you can go back to the real process to determine if the problem you are experiencing stems from there.

Once the team has gathered background information, the next step is determination of likely solutions (step 3).

23. View Problems as Opportunities and Mistakes as Progress

We tend to think of problems as just that—problems. But from another perspective, some could be opportunities. It's how we look at situations.

Figure 7-2. Scatter diagram.

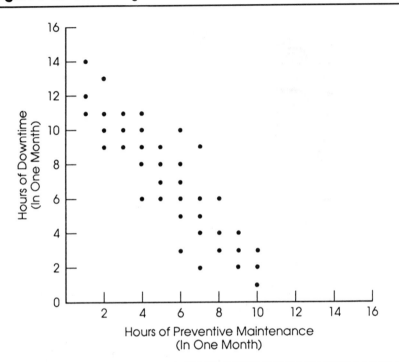

Source: Reprinted, by permission of publisher, from AMA MANAGEMENT BRIEFING, © 1993.
American Management Association, New York. All rights reserved.

Take what is happening to the publishing industry today. As we write this, more and more business periodicals are being discontinued because people read less than they used to and former readers now demand for immediate access to information. But looked at another way, the demise of management periodicals could mean the development of publications on audio and video cassette and on-line newsletters and books on CD-ROM. Mistakes in making the transition from print to Internet could be seen as learning experiences, progress toward more profitable products or marketplaces.

To see problems as opportunities, one has to be extremely open-minded in examining the problem and identifying a solution, not limited in one's thinking about a situation.

Most actual problem solving (step 4) is done with brainstorming. An individual on his own or a group of staff members attempts to identify as

Figure 7-3. Workflow diagram.

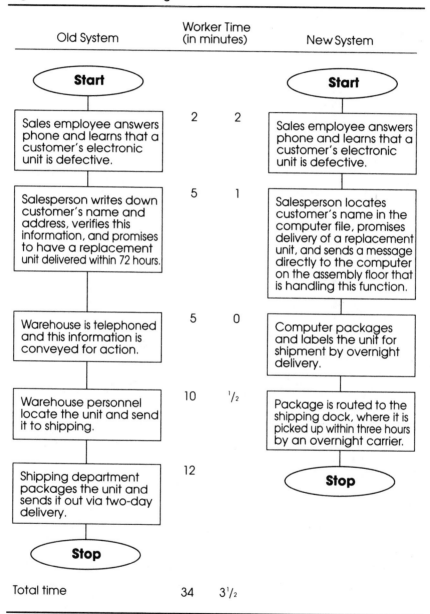

Old System	Worker Time (in minutes)		New System
Start			**Start**
Sales employee answers phone and learns that a customer's electronic unit is defective.	2	2	Sales employee answers phone and learns that a customer's electronic unit is defective.
Salesperson writes down customer's name and address, verifies this information, and promises to have a replacement unit delivered within 72 hours.	5	1	Salesperson locates customer's name in the computer file, promises delivery of a replacement unit, and sends a message directly to the computer on the assembly floor that is handling this function.
Warehouse is telephoned and this information is conveyed for action.	5	0	Computer packages and labels the unit for shipment by overnight delivery.
Warehouse personnel locate the unit and send it to shipping.	10	¹/₂	Package is routed to the shipping dock, where it is picked up within three hours by an overnight carrier.
Shipping department packages the unit and sends it out via two-day delivery.	12		**Stop**
Stop			
Total time	34	3¹/₂	

Figure 7-4. Cause and effect diagrams.

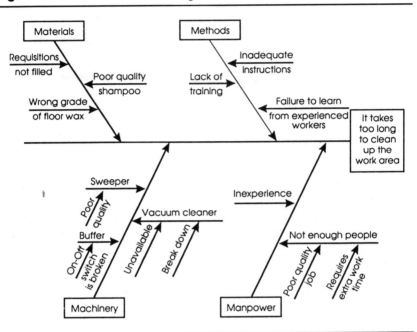

Source: Reprinted, by permission of publisher, from AMA MANAGEMENT BRIEFING, © 1993. American Management Association, New York. All rights reserved.

many solutions to a problem as possible. In the case of a group, members vocalize their thoughts as a member of the group lists them on a flip chart. No judgments are made until the brainstorming session is over.

If the group members are uncomfortable about calling out ideas, the leader might have members write their thoughts down on paper, then transfer these onto the flip chart. With all the team's ideas on the flip chart, the team is ready to move on to choose the best idea for implementation.

But there are other, lesser-known techniques that can help you look differently at problems—as opportunities—then identify ways to maximize the value of these opportunities.

Critical to doing this is how you define the problem. We've talked about the importance of defining the problem to avoid rushing to generate solutions before the problem has been clearly defined. One helpful bit of advice is to write a problem statement down. Begin it with the words "how to," then complete it with an appropriate verb. Naturally the verb you choose will influence how you see the problem, so a statement that begins "how to minimize" or "how to cope with" or "how to eliminate" sees the problem just as that, a problem, whereas a statement that begins "how to restore," "how to maximize," "how to gain" "how to accomplish," or "how to enhance" suggests a more positive view of the problem.

You might also take a statement like "how to cope with declining subscription sales," as in our earlier example of the publishing industry, and turn it on its head to "how to increase sales," then proceed from there. (Incidentally, the same can be done with an operational problem to gain new insights into potential solutions. You can take a problem like "how to decrease defect rate in products," turn it around to "how to increase defect rate," then list all the ways this could occur, ending up with a list of potential causes of the problem that might exist.)

Another technique would have the group look at a problem situation and identify those aspects of the problem that it likes—again in our publishing example, the growing numbers of people turning to new technology to get their information—thus allowing the group to focus on the real problem. It can then rewrite the problem statement. In our publishing example, it might be, "how to continue to provide information to our existing market."

24. Choose the Best Solution (Step 4)

If you can, in any problem-solving effort pretest your better ideas to identify the best. If you can't run small pilot tests first, then choose the best idea, adjusting it as circumstances require.

If you end up with several ideas, try multivoting, a technique in which the aim is to select the best idea in the opinion of the members: You review the ideas, link ideas where possible, then ask members to vote. Each time you vote, the list is reduced by half. In a short time, your list of fifty becomes a workable number for further study and final decision making.

If you have only a few ideas, you can vote to determine if you have consensus on one. Keep in mind that consensus doesn't require everyone to be in agreement—just that an idea be chosen that everyone can live with.

With an idea in mind, the next step is to develop a plan of action (step 5). That plan should specify what work still needs to be done and who "owns" what tasks associated with the mission. (Incidentally, "ownership" is an excellent phrase for the team to use in delegating tasks to members; it puts responsibility clearly on the person taking on the task.)

After all the preliminary work is done, the sixth and final step in problem solving is implementing the plan. Get senior management approval, if called for, to put your plan into action, monitoring the effort and making changes based on feedback.

25. Communicate Solutions

Solutions are valuable. Time spent in identifying and successfully implementing them gives them tremendous worth. They should never be hoarded. Rather, as a high-value manager, you know that they should be shared with other areas of the operation. This sharing can take place in management meetings, through the in-house newsletter, or one-on-one over lunch. Where a solution might truly benefit a colleague, you might even send a staff member to the peer's operation to work with that group to see that the idea is successfully implemented. Or your group might meet with the other department's staff to explain its accomplishments. Or you might set up a time to present the group's accomplishments, depending on how extensive the problem and solution are.

All these occasions give a high-value manager the opportunity not only to share the solution with colleagues, but to give recognition to those staff members who contributed significantly to the solution of the problem.

8

Focus on Customer Service and Quality Improvement

The high-value manager articulates the organization's beliefs about quality and service. But he or she does it in such a way that it becomes real to the employees. Perhaps the company has completed a survey of customers to determine their expectations. Sharing with employees the importance customers or clients place on service or quality by reporting on the survey results takes talk about quality out of the management fad category and makes it real. So does citing sales or other financial figures about the company and its competitors and the bottom-line impact of better quality or service. Show through survey data or operating statements the effect of value-added or enhanced service or product quality on customer attitudes and actions.

But in putting the spotlight on quality and customer service, high-value managers don't allow themselves to be blinded by an aspect of this Holy Grail of competitive success: Quality and value are not always synonymous. High-value managers recognize this. They don't, in the name of quality, allow efforts or resources to be expended that don't necessarily add value in the eyes of the customer. Too often, time is wasted or money is expended but to little consequence because the issue at which resources were thrown isn't perceived as worthwhile by the final judge on quality: the customer. High-value managers don't allow such situations to occur because they:

26. Determine customer needs, then develop action plans designed to achieve those needs. High-value managers don't try to guess what is important to the customer. They ask. Their understanding of customer value is based on surveys or focus groups they have conducted or a careful review of others' research.

27. Define "work quality" for their staff members. They might do this one-on-one, on the first day on the job or during the standard setting

phase of the performance evaluation program, or in a group setting, as in planning or problem solving. These standards provide guidelines that enable staff members to make decisions about how to use their time and other resources most productively.

28. Build individual and team pride in the work to support standards and decisions made about quality.

29. Live the message of quality, both its value and the danger of getting caught up in the chase.

26. Determine Customer Needs

It's easy for us to hypothesize about what our customers want, but are we necessarily right? Take Sue's case:

The Self-Centered Designer

Recently Sue was in a planning meeting discussing ways to increase sales of the company's fashion line. Sue is a designer, and when the facilitator asked Sue to define her customers' expectations and needs Sue seemed quite sure of herself as she answered "fashionable clothes" from high-quality textiles.

Sue's smile quickly turned to a frown when the facilitator asked her, "How do you know your customers want these things from your clothing line?" After some hemming and hawing, Sue admitted that that really was what she wanted from the clothing she purchased. The facilitator then asked, "Are you typical of your customers?"

Sue had to admit she wasn't. Further discussion determined that the company had last done a survey of its customers five years before and had never surveyed them on its new line of clothing. Given lack of knowledge, there was no way of knowing what impact Sue's ideas about the market's needs would have had on her company's bottom line. She felt the wearers of her designs would want the most expensive of materials, but in fact the firm's clients might have preferred sturdy materials that would allow for ease of laundering, which could have represented a considerable savings in production.

High-value managers would never find themselves in Sue's predicament. They regularly survey their customers. If they don't directly service external customers, and their customers instead are inside their organization, then they regularly meet with these individuals to be sure that their needs haven't changed and that they are still satisfied with the flow of work. If they make changes that demand more of their own staff's time, they check first to be sure that the changes are ones that will be welcomed by their internal customers because it will make their jobs easier. They don't make changes to improve quality, let alone changes for changes' sake, unless they are sure that these changes are worth the added effort or cost involved.

The same techniques used to survey external customers can be used to survey internal customers to identify those changes that will have value: telephone surveys, written questionnaires, and focus groups. At the very least, regularly call the head of the department for which you do work and ask, "How are we doing?" If you want more input, or your conversation suggests there might be a potential problem, you might suggest surveying the customer's department with a questionnaire you develop. The questionnaire might raise knotty questions about whether flow of work from your department creates downtime for your internal customer; your group's adherence to deadlines; the quality of the final product, including the rate of mistakes; and the level of customer satisfaction both with the work done and with interactions with members of your department. Focus groups, another approach, allow you to get a variety of opinions but in a more personal manner. The group could be made up of the head of the customer department and several of his or her staff members.

At the session, you might ask them to review work procedures to identify areas where improvements are possible that would make their own jobs easier. Bring along your key staff members to hear firsthand customer feedback. They, in turn, can share the feedback with the rest of your work group.

As an internal customer for another part of the organization, you might also want to initiate similar kinds of communications with those who supply you with work.

Parenthetically, recognize that these meetings are not one-time events. Customers' views on quality change, and consequently quality is not an end result but an ongoing process. High-value managers include on their to-do lists regular meetings with their customers to determine how the group's work is perceived. If it is an external customer, the high-value manager might visit with the customer, even see how his firm's product is being used, to get insights into what more can be done to satisfy the client. If it's an internal customer, a lunch or phone call every two months or so helps alert the high-value manager to any problems that exist between the two departments that might demand a reevaluation of the way work is being done.

27. Define "Work Quality" for Staff Members

Based on an understanding of customer needs, the high-value manager is able to be very specific about what quality work is. This helps empowered staff members make the best decisions about how they can best use their time. For instance, it might be worth it for a staff member in a legal office to proof a contract for a third time to be sure that there are no errors, but it might not be worth it for that same staff member to proof for typos a printed note from one attorney to another in the same office, particularly if it means that the paralegal will not have the time to finish some research for a court case to be heard the next day.

The kind of guidelines depends on the job and the individual's level of experience and need for supervision. Some staff members might have to know the basics—like what is "acceptable" work—whereas others might require only some clarification of work priorities and discussion of external or internal client needs. Where there is a need for specificity, the best place for it is as a part of the performance evaluation.

Depending on the job, you might indicate the number of acceptable errors or where and when shortcuts are allowed, or which issues of quality can *never* be ignored. These issues can also be addressed on the first day an employee joins your group, during the orientation, when he or she has no experiential background with which to make decisions about work quality or how to best use his or her time.

28. Build Individual and Team Pride

Staff members develop pride in their work and continue to improve its quality when they see their manager recognizing high-quality performance. High-value managers are always on the lookout for quality work by their staff members and praise them generously. But high-value managers make it a point to praise not only individual workers but the department as a whole whenever they can. They set quality goals that are challenging but within the work group's reach. When improvements are made within the department, they express appreciation during a staff meeting. How the improvement has helped all of the employees to accomplish their jobs easier and more efficiently is detailed. For example, a new filing system devised by a smart secretary might be showcased to all. The high-value manager might even demonstrate how much more easily documents can be found and retrieved.

Where quality improvements have had a direct improvement on production or sales, the manager hangs a chart that displays the slow but steady steps the group is making toward achieving its quality standards. Perhaps the head of the department experiencing the benefits of the group's quality efforts is invited to attend a staff meeting and personally compliment the group on its efforts. Successful managers demonstrate they trust their own employees by encouraging them to do their periodic checks on their own work and even to inspect each others' work—a second pair of eyes can detect errors that might otherwise be missed.

The high-value manager also demonstrates his or her pride in the work group by bringing them together to address and identify solutions to questions like the following:

- How satisfied are *we* with the quality of work *we* produced for our customers?
- Has our department changed any of its methods for doing its work in the past two years?
- Are there ways we could do the work that would decrease the current rate of mistakes or better meet others' deadlines or improve the quality of the work we do to both our satisfaction and our internal customers' satisfaction?

High-value managers believe: Measure how well your department is doing, improve it, then measure it again. Techniques described in Chapter 7 may help to identify root causes of problems in product quality or service. In the process of problem solving, the group may identify policies, procedures, equipment, or work conditions that inhibit quality service or product. Small changes in these not only might make a difference, but a high-value manager's willingness to change them demonstrates that he or she is truly committed to improving quality.

How successful are you in making quality happen in your operation? Ask yourself these questions:

- Do you establish quality responsibilities and expectations with each staff member?

- Have you talked with your employees about the other employees and departments within your organization that rely on their work and what those other employees and departments expect?
- Do you get feedback from external or internal customers and share this information with your staff?
- Do you encourage your staff to assess their efforts in meeting the quality standards and expectations you set?
- Do you review their efforts in the area of quality at the performance evaluation interview at the end of the year, including any problems they encountered that made it difficult to exceed expectations?
- Even if you have no direct contact with external customers, do you translate corporate beliefs into actions to enable your staff to improve the quality of their work?
- Do you begin each new year, as a part of the performance appraisal program, with a goal and an action plan to ensure further quality development over the next twelve months?

"Yes" answers to these questions suggest that you are creating a high-quality work environment.

29. Lead by Example

The high-value manager demonstrates, in deed, the importance of quality service and product. The successful manager keeps a sharp vigilance on slippage in work quality and does not accept it as inevitable. He or she knows that ignoring these slight slippages sends a message to the staff that quality is only being given lip service, that it is truly not important to the person in charge. So, when quality problems arise, the high-value manager speaks to those responsible immediately and strongly and makes it clear that quality standards must be met consistently.

He or she isn't focused only on this negative side of the quality equation. On the positive side, besides giving recognition when individuals or the team as a whole exceeds the group's definition of quality, a high-value manager makes changes in operations based on staff member suggestions. High-value managers actively listen to employees when they complain about worn-out equipment or problems with the lighting or some procedure. They recognize that their employees are closer to the problems, and their ideas can often make the operation more efficient and less expensive while improving the quality of the end product.

Quality improvements made by employees are also rewarded with new and challenging assignments, preferably ones in which the employees can use new skills and in which they are interested.

High-value managers also demonstrate by their actions that they are not excused from treating their internal customers as courteously and carefully as they do outside customers. No member of the work group is allowed to be impolite to someone from another area of the business or to think he or she can take a rough day out on a peer from somewhere else in the company. And that includes the group's leader. That courtesy rule applies even when the group member or leader is dealing with someone the group considers a pest. Note, for example, how one high-value manager, Phil, dealt with an irate customer:

Cooling a Cranky Customer

When Phil became head of Systems, his staff expected him to easily lose his cool when dealing with Mindy, a department head. Phil had a temper, and he admitted to it, but he told his staff that he had learned to keep it in check whenever dealing with internal clients. But Mindy had built a reputation in Systems for being a real pest: She was forever calling to complain about some problem with her software or hard drive. If it wasn't stack overflow problems, it was a virus, and if it wasn't a virus, it was a network malfunction. Often there *was* a problem, but what annoyed the systems group was Mindy's unpleasant demeanor when they arrived, and her know-it-all attitude as they tried to explain to her the cause of the difficulty.

"Wait until Phil meets Mindy," Stan told Betty over lunch. "Well, it's likely to be this afternoon," she answered. "We were so tied up with that network mess in Marketing that I didn't have a chance to get back to her when she called the help line this morning. She's likely to come marching into Systems demanding attention as soon as she comes back from lunch. I know she's not in right now because I called, and her assistant said she had left for a lunch date furious because she couldn't use her PC.

As Betty had predicted, Mindy was striding in front of them, heading for Systems, as Stan and Betty returned from the company cafeteria. Mindy hadn't even waited to remove her coat.

"So you're the new head of Systems," she said to Phil in a voice that suggested she was there to fight.

"Hi," said Phil. "I'm sorry I haven't had a chance to meet with all users, but we have had some major problems since I arrived, and—"

"You didn't think my problems were important enough, is that it?" Mindy interrupted.

Phil paused for a moment, smiled, then asked, "What is the problem?" He then listened as Mindy identified about ten difficulties either with her department's network or her own PC. He told her, "Some of those problems require Systems support, but others could be handled by your own staff once they become more familiar with aspects of the network. Why don't we sit down and discuss how we can best address your needs?"

There was a noticeable thaw in Mindy's manner. "Well, yes, I'd appreciate that," she said. Then she and Phil spent two hours discussing some of the shortfalls in her department's system. To improve the quality of work, she offered some ideas that would have proven costly. Phil agreed that the improvements would do what she wanted but they also might create problems for staff because they demanded skills beyond those her staff currently had. "Maybe we can make these improvements in stages," he suggested. "I would also like to begin some in-house training, starting with your department. Once we get started and they get more comfortable with the new software, your employees likely will be able to set up their own users' group in which members help each other out."

Mindy felt that she had finally been heard. Phil's suggestions would provide higher productivity at less additional Systems costs, and her staff—and Mindy herself, she admitted to Phil—would learn how to better use the technology.

Phil's staff was surprised. Afterwards, Phil told them, "None of us should lose our tempers with our internal clients. We have a tough job, with all the new technology this company expects us to install and get operational, but we have to understand that end users have their problems, too, and we have to focus on their needs."

Over the next week, Phil spent several hours with Mindy developing a course curriculum for her staff. In the end, Mindy became one of the strongest supporters of the systems group, singing their praises to all.

How did Phil accomplish what his staff felt was a miracle? Most important, he did what he had told his staff they should always do: He treated her with courtesy.

In dealing with an irate customer, high-value managers also know you need to:

- *Focus on the customer.* Clear your mind of any distractions that might keep you from concentrating totally on the customer's needs. Customers recognize when your mind is elsewhere. They are likely to calm down when they see you have gone out of your way to give them your undivided attention.

- *Stay objective.* Phil had heard about Mindy from his predecessor, so he was forewarned. But to deal successfully with an irate customer, the best advice is to keep your emotions under control. Don't let the customer's negative comments affect your attitude or judgment.

- *Listen.* Phil is a high-value manager, skilled at active listening. He listened to Mindy's complaints with an open mind, and that allowed him to recognize what she really needed, not necessarily what she thought she should have in the way of new systems equipment and software. Because he didn't interrupt her, Mindy was also able to vent some of her anger. This can diffuse pent-up emotion and make a difficult customer less demanding.

- *Use feedback.* "Uh huh" or "go on" may be all a customer needs to know that you are paying attention.

- *Paraphrase.* After listening to Mindy's myriad demands, Phil restated, in his own words, what he had heard. Again, it proved to Mindy that she was being listened to. But it also reassured her that Phil understood her problem, and it helped her to feel that he really cared about her dilemma.

- *Ask questions.* Finally, before agreeing to Mindy's demands, Phil asked questions to be sure that he understood why she was so upset. Open-ended questions helped him to determine that the course of action she was proposing would increase the quality of her systems but have little value in improving the quality of the work or the productivity of her work group.

You train staff members to deal with irate external or internal customers this way, but more important you model this behavior yourself when faced with a problem situation. You know how a team emulates its leader.

To sum up, what makes a quality effort? As a high-value manager, you know it is one based on:

- *Research first.* Acquire information about your customers' needs and wants. Share research data or financial information from your own firm or competitors' that shows the impact of quality or better service on customer sales.

- *Comparison of other operations.* If possible, benchmark your department's quality performance against departments in competitor organizations or the best-run organizations.

- *Brainstorming with staff.* The staff should have individual quality requirements but there should also be work group goals, and the staff should meet to identify ways to achieve these goals.

- *Monitoring of progress.* Attend to problems in quality as soon as they arise. Be ready to make changes when needed. If the problem is related to either a staff shortage or need for new equipment or technology, do a cost-benefit analysis to be sure that the quality that will be achieved will have value. If so, then get what your staff needs to do the best-quality job possible.

- *Feedback.* Consistently recognize individual and team successes. If employees run into problems, coach and counsel them to correct the problem. Also, apply the feedback process to internal customers. When you have made changes in the procedures or operations to increase quality, check with customers to see that these changes have had the desired results.

- *Reinforcement.* Besides reminding employees of the need for quality, the leader has to practice what he or she preaches. We know a manager who could either send out a mediocre product or absorb the additional expense of last-minute improvements in a product in order to produce a higher-quality product for customers. The manager believed the changes made the product significantly safer, so he chose to absorb the additional expense rather than produce shoddy merchandise. Incidentally, the value-added quality for the parents of the kids who used the toy produced led to sales way above those of competitors. Which showed staff that quality pays off not only in better customer relations but on the bottom line.

- *Celebration of success and the tackling of new objectives.* Like we said, quality is ongoing. While celebrating achievement of quality standards, you should be setting new goals and tackling new problems to continue to increase product or service quality.

9

Managing the White Spaces

As companies downsize, solid or dotted lines on organization charts lead nowhere. Layoffs, reorganizations, or restructuring leaves white spaces within departments or between groups. Within these white spaces may be problems or opportunities that previously were someone's responsibility but now don't officially belong to anyone. Or these orphan tasks might stem from recent changes in the technology available to the firm, the marketplace in which it sells its products, or the distribution channels by which it sells them—they may not be problems but rather opportunities that the company is not availing itself of because no one fully knows their worth.

The situation is understandable. It's tough enough for managers to complete their assigned work in today's leaner organizations, let alone address situations for which they have no responsibility. Everyone is so busy that it's easy to think of orphan responsibilities as someone else's job. Consequently, tasks that exist in the white space frequently go unattended.

Some orphans are like gnats, annoying but deserving of nothing more than a swat of the hand. If it was clear whom these orphans belonged to, they might find themselves at the bottom of that individual manager's priorities list. But some orphans hold the potential for significantly increasing corporate revenue or decreasing expenses.

As a high-value manager, you:

30. Recognize orphans for what they are.

31. Know how to make judgments about which orphans or problems in white space to devote time to.

32. Draw attention to the orphan or problem without invading another person's turf.

33. Encourage staff members to step into the white space to benefit the department or organization as a whole, and do so yourself.

34. Build synergy by bringing together colleagues to work on the issue. Open communications and begin spanning the white space between job titles or departments.

30. Recognize Orphans

We all have clear-cut responsibilities. In more traditional organizations they are a part of job descriptions. Our boundaryless organizations depend more on ongoing communications to clarify those tasks that *must* be accomplished. But as we do our work, we often find areas not being attended to. These unattended areas can be extremely frustrating when they affect our own performance. There is the desire to blame some colleague for not fully doing his or her job. We walk away annoyed, feeling that we aren't able to do our own work because of someone else's imperfect job performance.

High-value managers aren't so quick to prejudge or walk away. Rather than spend their time venting about a peer's failure to hold up his or her end of the work, they investigate to determine who would be responsible for that area of the operation. They then bring the problem to the attention of their colleague, and together they address the situation that is negatively influencing their own efforts.

If accountability isn't clear, the high-value manager goes to his own supervisor to learn who is responsible for that area of the operation. Once the manager finds out whose jurisdiction the task falls under, he phones or visits with the person. This isn't a time for finger-pointing or accusations that someone is not holding up his end of the work. High-value managers know that only causes defensive behavior and counteraccusations that the high-value manager is minding other people's business. Forget that the individual's neglect of an operational area is causing the high-value manager problems.

Curing a Computer Virus

Let's assume that a computer virus problem is running rampant in the high-value manager's department, causing computer downtime and loss of work in progress. Pete, from the systems group, was responsible for doing monthly checks on all PCs to determine the existence of viruses. He also was investigating a means of protecting the high-value manager's network from viral infestations. Then he left to become an independent consultant. Money is tight so Pete's job has not been filled.

Sue, our high-value manager, believes that this part of Pete's job should have been delegated to another staff member, or outsourced, until Systems could hire a full-time staff member. She's upset but brings up the problem in a low-key manner. She tells Joe, the head of Systems, "I've noticed that nobody is in charge of seeing that our antiviral programs are updated since Pete left, and I will bet that some of the systems problems people are experiencing would disappear if someone were in charge." Sue then waits to see if Joe reacts. If Joe agrees that it is a problem and offers to look into the matter, maybe delegate it to one of his staff members, Sue has accomplished her objective. It doesn't matter who handles the orphan task so long as the problem is resolved. And if Joe gets praised for assigning a staff member to complete Pete's research to install an antiviral network device, he might even credit Sue. "Well, it was really Sue's idea."

But if Joe doesn't take up the challenge, then Sue knows it is up to her to get the job done if the problem her work group is experiencing is to end. Sue might meet with her own supervisor again and discuss the possibility of contracting out the task to Pete until such time as Systems has restaffed Pete's old job.

But, as we said, not all orphans can demand outlays of time or money when both are short in most companies.

If you discover a problem or situation and the manager or group that normally would be responsible for it refuses to assume that responsibility, you shouldn't just seize the initiative and run with it. While ensuring installation of an antiviral program is one thing, there are many other orphan tasks that can be left alone without any damage to the organization or loss of revenue. If we rushed off to do every task that we would like to do, we would have no time to do those tasks that *must* be done.

A high-value manager pauses before acting in order to determine how much time, if any, to invest personally in dealing with an orphan task. Since orphans can crop up daily in the course of work, high-value managers may even have to jot down a description of them when they encounter them in order not to forget any. Some may be picked up by their rightful parents, but others may depend on you to nurture. But before you do you need to measure the cost of involvement against the benefit of return.

31. Know Which Orphans to Adopt

It's easy to be enticed into the white space to take on a task that no one else is addressing, particularly if we think tending to this orphan could bring us some prestige or add to the bottom line. But high-value managers hold back and first do mental calculations, if not paper ones, on the value of working either on their own or with others on the orphan task. The orphan must make their own work easier or bring in additional revenue. Since attempting to solve an orphan problem or mine an orphan opportunity could be seen as infringing on another manager's territory, the high-value manager needs to be sure that the orphan is worth the time that might have to be spent on organizational diplomacy. Orphans may take minimal managerial effort but demand tremendous patience in dealing with individuals who suddenly see their turf being invaded if the orphan will gain them high visibility or a better operating report.

It helps in analyzing orphans if a manager has an understanding of other departments' missions and objectives. Knowledge of disciplines other than his or her own—even a superficial knowledge—also helps the high-value manager to gauge the orphan's benefit to the organization and who else's expertise may be called for to make the potential of the orphan a reality.

> Recently Carol, who heads up her firm's baby foods product group, was in planning with her staff members. One member pointed out the growing concern parents had about how healthy the firm's baby food was. The group began to brainstorm and came up with the idea of a brand of baby food that had little salt and no added sugar and was cholesterol free. The product would satisfy mothers' desire to start their children off as soon as possible on a healthy diet, but the staff wasn't sure how successful such a line of food would be. It didn't fit into its current line of canned or bottled baby foods, and there was another product group that offered healthy cuisine for adults, AdultDiets. Was this an area that AdultDiet planned to pursue? Carol's group didn't know.

Fortunately Carol was aware of a recent study done by the AdultDiet group. Study findings showed growing concern among adults about the entire family's health. The AdultDiet group had seen the survey results as a green flag to extend their line of foods to include teen treats but had no plans to enter the baby food market. Besides, Carol reasoned, her group had as much right to pursue the idea as did the Adult-Diet group, which wouldn't have the resources to explore this product area for at least two years while Carol's group had the resources to do so now.

Carol was also familiar with the AdultDiet group's distribution channels from her attendance at managers' meetings, so she knew that there would be shelf space for the baby food her group was proposing to develop and sell without cutting into shelf space for either AdultDiet's current line of packaged food or its new line of healthy teen snacks.

Consultation with her marketing manager convinced both the marketing manager and Carol that the dollar return was well worth pursuing this orphan, although they both also knew that Carol's counterpart in charge of the AdultDiet line might see Carol's new product entry as invading her marketplace.

Summing up, because of organizational white space, and the orphans floating within it, it helps a manager to have:

- *Organizational knowledge.* You need to know other groups' strategic goals or plans as well as your own and the corporate direction.

- *Understanding of the entire organization.* You or your boss needs to know who is responsible for what. This allows you to go to the correct person when you spot a problem not being addressed. Then you can either leave that area knowing it will be resolved or, if no one wants responsibility for it, you may have to assume responsibility if you want something done about the situation.

- *Good time-management skills.* You need to be sure that you won't be neglecting more important tasks to devote time to the orphan. Or you must have an action plan that will allow you to delegate some of your own tasks to free yourself to work either alone or with others on a profit-making orphan.

32. Avoid Political Problems

Admittedly, white spaces can be politically sensitive areas to enter. But it is also true that in today's leaner organizations these white spaces are more likely to exist. And as a manager, you have to enter them and work with colleagues to address the orphan tasks you find there, even colleagues like Clara.

Dealing with a Turf Watchdog

Clara is Carol's counterpart, and she is a watchdog when it comes to protecting her turf. Carol knew that she would have to move cautiously to pursue this product idea without creating problems that might end up delaying entry into this potentially profitable market, let alone derailing an opportunity for her own product line.

Carol had done some soul searching, and she admitted that she was excited by the idea of being in charge of the first products to enter this market, but she also was willing to allow Clara's group to have the idea if AdultDiet could have product on shelf within twelve months. So at the next managers' meeting, Carol asked Clara if she would like to look at some numbers she and her marketing manager had developed about the importance parents placed on good diet for their toddlers. She said, "Clara, have you thought about how AdultDiet could be targeted to babies' needs?"

"Why do you ask?" Clara asked suspiciously. "Well," said Carol, reaching for air, "we were discussing the issue during planning. I wondered if you had thought about it."

"Not really," said Clara. "Besides, right now we have our hands full with these line extensions we're developing."

"I realize that," said Carol. "I know right now you are without a marketing manager, and I wondered if Becky could help you by doing some of the number crunching your group will need to submit its business plan."

"That would really be great," said Clara, still suspicious. "Had your group plans on entering the health food area?" Carol could see the battle lines being drawn. What should she say next that would gain her the benefit of Clara's experience in this marketplace yet still allow the company to introduce the line of baby food within the next twelve months?

Carol said, "Yes, we did have such plans, and we thought you would want to be involved in product development and delivery. We know you have other coals in the fire right now, and probably have little time to involve yourself or group fully in another product idea, but you could bring on board a lot of information my group lacks. With members of both your and my team working together, we could get a product on grocery shelves in nine months if we were lucky."

Carol realized that the keys to operating within the white space with Clara were (1) asking questions, not making statements, to tie Clara's need to hers, and (2) requesting Clara's help.

To the surprise of other managers who overhead the exchange, as well as perhaps of Carol, Clara agreed to work with Carol's group to produce the special line of baby food.

Let's look at what would have happened if Clara had argued that the product really belonged to her group. What should Carol have done then? She should have backed off after being assured that Clara would indeed be able to bring this new product to market within the timeline necessary to make the most of its introduction. To be sure of that, she could have offered to lend staff knowledgeable about the baby food market to Clara to see that the project moved along, even volunteered her own time to work under Clara's leadership as the company worked to put its new line in mothers' shopping carts.

High-value managers are team players. They don't pursue orphan tasks for the visibility it might give them but rather for the contribution that the truly valuable ones will make in their organization's bottom line. While they may get credit for picking up a ball no one else owns, or whose last owner is no longer with the company, their objective has to be to benefit their organization. Since the tending to orphans often means spanning departments or other groups, a manager never should go into an orphan-related project with the intention of hogging all the credit.

33. Encourage Employee Initiative

Since staff members may also identify orphans within either the department or company in the course of their work, the high-value manager needs to empower employees to get out of their boxes and work on these orphans either to make their own work easier or add to the bottom line of the operating statement. Staff should advise their manager of any orphans they encounter, discuss their action plan—since there may be political minefields that their manager can advise them about—then be allowed to pursue the orphan, particularly if it represents a good opportunity for the organization. High-value managers never say, "That's beyond our responsibility." Or, "Shouldn't that be something the Connecticut branch should be doing?" Or, "We're doing all right without that."

Here are some other answers that high-value managers know never to use with employees who bring them ideas that don't fit within the organization's mission yet could help out the department or the organization:

"Don't be ridiculous!"
"You don't have the time."
"That's not our problem."
"Let's get back to reality."
"But we would have to change your description to . . ."
"It's not a part of our plans for the year; maybe in a year or two we could do something about it."

We have a friend who works for a manager who is always encouraging his staff members to step out of the box, but each time they do and present him with their ideas they hear one or more of these responses. White space now frightens them. They do what is written in their job description and nothing more.

34. Build Synergy

When orphan tasks are encountered, the most effective way to handle them without stirring up political troubles is to span organizational boundaries, bringing in individuals from groups that might be responsible for some orphan to work together on the project.

Staff members with strong social skills as well as solid technical or other professional skills might be best suited to serve as department liaison on orphan projects. They can represent the department in group meetings or otherwise span the white space between departments.

Spanning Departmental Borders

Walter is a believer in spanning organizational borders. Aware of the white space that floats between departments, Walter has assigned the task of liaison to his assistant manager. His assistant is responsible for meeting each month with groups the department works with to determine areas either where Walter's group is not serving the client well or where opportunities for cooperative efforts exist. Walter also encourages staff members to participate in efforts outside that have nothing to do with their job descriptions. We know one such employee, and she is forever praising Walter for his willingness to allow her to get outside her box to work with others within the organization on mutual problems or opportunities. Because his staff know how Walter feels about border spanning, in planning they will bring orphans to his attention and offer to enter the white space and cooperate or coordinate with other groups. Their successes gain recognition at the quarterly staff meetings he holds, the news sheet he sends throughout the organization that lets the management staff know what his group is doing—so they can sign on to projects that interest them—and in performance evaluations.

Walter recently extended his span of control, absorbing another product line, and since white space currently exists between the two groups he is encouraging cross-functional brainstorming sessions to identify and solve white-space problems. Besides generating a variety of good ideas that either or both groups can work on, such sessions allow him and staff members from both teams to make suggestions without seeming like they are invading another person's territory.

High-value managers sometimes form continuous improvement teams made up of managers from a variety of operating areas to work on all white-space problems. The group begins with a single problem and, if it is successful, they continue to meet to address other problems brought to their attention either by members of the group or senior management.

In the next section of this book, we will address in detail how to successfully use teams.

Section IV
Teams and Team Management

If there is one major shift in the way in which work is accomplished today, it is in the extensive use of teams. They are being used at every level of the organization—from the office or factory floor to executive row. Their objective may be to reduce costs or to increase productivity, to develop new products or services, to increase customer service or quality.

Some organizations have gone beyond using teams to accomplish a single mission. Rather, they have torn down department walls and erected in their place process teams made up of individuals from different disciplines who now work together on an ongoing basis. Given the level of team activity within most companies, we could almost guarantee that within the next twenty-four hours you will either be asked to join a team, attend a team meeting, or decide to form a team of your own to solve some problem or accomplish some other goal.

Despite the extensive literature on teams, many managers still have not developed the skills they need to lead teams effectively. Since the objectives of many team efforts are critical to the organization's bottom line, and consequently senior management is focused on these efforts, failure as a team or project leader can have significant career implications.

Given those implications, high-value managers know that the stakes are high in team participation, whatever the team's mission. Consequently they master team leadership and facilitation. They know how to represent their team before senior management, how to coach and counsel members of the team—even peers—without alienating them, in order to achieve the team's mission, and how to make the team experience a positive one by seeing that the time members spend in teams is productive. If there is one complaint we have heard from managers about being a part of a team, it is the frustration that comes from making the time for a team effort that comes to naught.

We've divided the core competencies for team leadership into five categories to help you better understand your new role as team leader. Make no mistake. You will find more of your time spent in team meetings. Make it time well spent for you and your colleagues.

10

Team Facilitation

We've long heard about the benefits of teamwork, about managers who can make their staffs think as a team. But now, as continuous improvement efforts are taking root in companies, department boundaries are falling down. Managers are expected to collaborate on teams, just as employees in the same department are expected to work as a team for greater productivity.

Teams and your participation in them may occur in a number of ways.

- A member of senior management may ask you to head a task force.
- A manager may ask you to join a long-standing or new team in which your experience or knowledge would be essential.
- You may see a problem within your department, and you may assign individuals on staff, or ask for volunteers, to work together to address the situation. The team would be self-managed, and you, as sponsor, would provide the group with guidance from a distance.
- You may see a corporate problem that needs to be addressed and get top-management approval to set up a managerial team to solve the problem. In such a situation, a senior manager might serve as "sponsor" or team mentor, helping to get the team the financial and other resources it will need to succeed.

If you are to participate effectively in a team, you need to know how to facilitate the team process, to make the discussion and problem-solving and decision process flow more smoothly, in order to bring about change in the form of new products or improved operations. High-value managers are successful heads of teams, members of teams, and/or sponsors of self-directed teams because they:

35. Know the various stages in which teams operate, their responsibilities in each, and they anticipate potential problems to prevent them from becoming real ones.

36. Know if a team is truly warranted. High-value managers know that some problems are better handled by a manager working alone or one-on-one with another associate.

37. Know about the latest technology so you can reduce the need to bring in experts from other organization sites, thus saving work time and travel expenses.

38. Be able to staff a team with the right members and gain their support and cooperation, even when they oversee other departments or functions within the organization.

39. Define the team's mission and its goals and stay on that track through completion of the project.

40. Run meetings smoothly by setting ground rules for communication and behavior within the team structure.

41. Intervene when communication and behavior problems arise. High-value managers know that some members of a team can be silenced if they feel their ideas will be put down, their views will be belittled, or their comments denigrated.

35. The Stages of a Team Project

If you are a high-value manager, you need to understand those stages through which a team goes. There are four.

The first stage is *forming,* during which the team mission is finalized and members agree about what is acceptable team behavior. While there may be some disagreements over leadership and team governance, most differences will focus on team mission but they will be usually nonconfrontational.

The second stage—*storming*—is the phase in which conflicts between members are more likely to arise. As ideas are shared and action plans are developed, proprietary feelings arise about people's ideas and turf. Aware of such problems' likelihood, high-value managers usually exert greater control during this phase of the team process. Knowledgeable about which members bring sensitive egos to the group, they are more responsive to member needs for recognition. Thus this stage is not traumatic for team members led by a high-value manager.

During the third phase—*norming*—group members really get down to business. They take on informal roles as well as formal assignments. For instance, one member might emerge as an organizational leader, skilled at determining what needs to get done and when, and able to get everyone pulling in the right direction. You might even want to assign this person to do post-meeting coordination, following up with members to be sure that they are completing their assignments on schedule. Another member might emerge as a writer/reporter, not only keeping the group's minutes but taking on a major role in the writing of the final white paper issued by the group.

Still another member might become an information gatherer, searching for facts and other information to help the team in its problem-sensing stage. Yet another member might act as peacekeeper, helping the leader reconcile disputes and disagreements.

Many members prove themselves to be quiet followers, and the high-value leader knows that a key responsibility to these team members is to provide a supportive environment in which they will feel comfortable sharing their ideas and opinions.

As members play to each other's strengths and work in concert, the team enters the fourth and final phase of team management, *performing.* This phase ends in completion of the team project.

36. Know If a Team Is Needed

While teams seem to be the new way to get work done within organizations, high-value managers realize that they aren't the only way to accomplish objectives.

If you or a staff member, working independently, could accomplish the same goal, there is no point in setting up a team just to get input from others. That can be handled via telephone, on E-mail, or by a one-on-one meeting in the office or over lunch. It's even possible today to get a group together on a corporate network for a one-time exchange of information to solve a problem or get information to make a decision. The decision itself and implementation of that decision may not demand a group effort.

Enough of managers' time is spent in meetings as is. High-value managers create teams only where the individuals can bring together a variety of perspectives that will contribute to a better idea and where integration of different knowledge and skills can both open networks of information not available to a single manager and increase acceptance and therefore successful implementation of the final idea.

37. Using Technology

For the same reason that teams aren't always the only method of resolving a problem or making a decision, so meetings of a group are not the only way in which members of a team can get together. And high-value managers recognize this.

Today, given the technology available, you don't have to have all members of a team in the same room to hold a meeting, which saves time and dollars in travel costs, plus expands your choice of individuals for membership in a team. Membership doesn't have to be limited to only those who are located at your site or facility.

We recently worked on a team in which several members were hooked by phone line to the meeting room, thereby allowing these long-distance members to attend meetings regularly without leaving their off-site locations. But phone isn't the only way to link members at different sites.

Videoconferencing and interactive networks are other options open.

Unlike audioconferences, which don't allow you to monitor body language or facial cues, videoconferencing allows you to watch member reactions to comments as well as hear their responses. The technology is now available and the larger companies usually have videoconferencing capability at least at headquarters or overseas sites.

Interactive networks are another way for team members to communicate with each other without leaving their work location. Members sit at computer terminals and input their ideas or decision on an issue. The individuals' responses are integrated by the hardware and software and shown on a screen at the front of the room(s).

These systems are increasingly being used for both problem solving and product development. While some people complain that the technology is too impersonal, those who use it for product development and problem solving support its use because it encourages greater team participation. Ideas can be submitted anonymously, as can negative feedback to an idea or proposal, thereby increasing team participation.

But however you plan to get your group together, the first step is to identify team members.

38. Identifying the Right People for the Team

The purpose of the group plays a major factor in team selection. Will it solely provide feedback to others? Will it have a specific project to complete? Will you need a small project team of expert technicians or will you require a larger group, with a broad range of backgrounds represented, for brainstorming? Answers to these questions will help you narrow your selection.

Generally, in selecting team members, high-value managers look for people with both knowledge in their functional areas and strong interpersonal skills, although they are realistic enough to set aside people skills if a project has a strong technical bias. If the project calls for a major shift in organizational direction, successful managers know, too, they will be better off with people who are unafraid of change than with individuals with caretaker mentalities.

Needless to say, a team leader wants individuals who are interested enough in a project to give sufficient time to it. If a prospective member doesn't see participation as a worthwhile challenge, then another candidate is better for consideration. High-value managers also look for diversity in putting together their team. Limiting the group to people with interests similar to one's own would be limiting the final result as well.

High-value managers know the importance of having creative thinkers on their team, but they don't go only for the hotshot ideators. You should have more-traditional problem solvers as well on board. The best teams are those made up of both types of individuals. Creative innovators may give you an out-of-the-box idea but may not have the patience to hang in there during implementation that adapters or modifiers have. The latter are also more likely to find ways to make those breakthrough ideas work!

Further, bringing highly creative individuals who only think out of the box into a project whose purpose is continuous improvement will only frustrate the creative persons because their approach to problem solving goes far beyond the goal of the project. And, conversely, bringing on board too many problem solvers for a new product-oriented project will tend to frustrate both the creative innovators who will feel the creative process is being stymied and the adaptors who will feel inadequate and underappreciated when their ideas are ignored because they don't go far enough outside the box.

How will you know who specifically is best to choose for your team?

If the team is made up of people from your own department, then your choice is easier since you know who is capable of doing what and how much time each individual can spare to the effort. But it's more likely that the team you will head will be made up of other managers or those who work for other managers. Then you need to talk to their supervisors to determine who within the supervisors' department has the needed people and/or technical skills, who would work best in groups, and who can be spared and for how long.

Ask your own staff as well whom they would recommend to be a part of the team.

Crossing department boundaries to get participation in teams from staff or managers of other departments isn't always easy. When a project calls for cross-functional participation, you may need first to get the other department to buy into your team's objective or mission by demonstrating how the other department can benefit from participation in the project.

39. Defining Mission and Goals

Clarification of mission is as important to team success as proper selection of team membership. The team needs a clear sense of what it will be doing.

While you may have given members broad guidelines about the team's objectives at the time of recruitment, that mission and the date by which it must be achieved need to be finalized by the group. The first two or so meetings of the team can be spent doing this. In setting a time frame for completion of the team objective, keep in mind that members have full-time jobs and will have to find time in their busy schedules to work on team assignments. So be realistic in setting project due dates.

A well-written mission statement—and it should be written—includes the reasons for the team's existence and the limits of its authority. Don't be too concerned if you have to spend several sessions on the group's mission. There should be no confusion among members about the purpose of their efforts. A high-value manager recognizes the value of all agreeing on their destination in setting out on a course. It lessens the need for course corrections—and makes them easier when they are called for.

In defining the team's mission and goals, your goal as a high-value manager, as in most team issues, is to reach consensus, not necessarily unanimity. Consensus simply means that not everyone agrees with a decision but everyone can live with that decision.

Framing the mission statement and hanging it in the room in which the team regularly meets serves to keep the team on track and provides a yardstick against which members' plans and actions can be assessed. Actually, if possible, a room should be dedicated to the team where members can work on the project at any time during the day. A high-value manager knows that the more opportunities members have to spend together, the better the rapport among them. And informal exchanges can stimulate brainstorming that carries over into team meetings.

40. Run Meetings Smoothly

Having a clearly defined mission isn't the only clarification needed early on in a team effort. Steve's case gives us insight into another key factor in team success:

Chairing a Team the Wrong Way

For over a year, Steve has been chairing a team whose purpose is to address customers' environmental demands. To date, very little has been accomplished. To understand why, consider what happened recently when the group met to discuss a mailing to its clients.

Steve needed to have the group approve the final mailing piece. He thought he would need the team members for about fifteen to thirty minutes, and he was at the conference room promptly at two. No one showed until after two-fifteen. By two-thirty, it became obvious that half the group wasn't coming, including some key people whose technical knowledge was critical to the review of the promotional copy. Phone calls helped to capture two members; Steve's secretary reported that the others were with clients or otherwise tied up.

Steve decided to proceed only to be confronted by angry complaints by the two last-minute arrivals that they had never been notified about the meeting and angry retorts by those who had arrived earlier about the time they had wasted in waiting to get down to work. Worse, later that day, Steve was castigated by those who hadn't been able to make the meeting about his poor planning and organization. But during the meeting itself, the discord went from bad to worse, as the members took their anger out on the task at hand, nitpicking over the mailing piece. Steve could not quell the complaints; turf battles occurred, and one member after another tried to dominate the team session, while the two creators of the mail piece whispered to one another.

Steve has trouble grasping why his team is so fractious, but clearly a contributing problem, if not the major problem, is that at no point early on did Steve and his group set operational ground rules for their meetings. Such ground rules could have covered not only when and where the group would meet—as well as the handling of last-minute get-togethers—but how discussions would be controlled and how disruptive behavior would be handled.

Among the questions that such ground rules should address are:

- Where and when will meetings be held?
- How will emergency meetings be handled?
- How long will meetings last?
- How will decisions be reached?
- How will the team network with others within the organization?
- How will the team report to the sponsor or senior management?
- How will the team handle conflicts and disagreements among its members?
- Will the team evaluate each session after the fact to help improve subsequent sessions?

The high-value manager works with the team to set ground rules. To stimulate discussion, he or she might come with some questions prepared in advance. For instance, a team leader might ask the group, "What was a major problem with the last team project you worked on? What could we do to avoid that problem this time?" Or, "How can be we sure that we are focused on the team's mission?" Or, "What rules will enable us to manage the discussions without controlling the flow of ideas or information?"

High-value managers certainly do not come to a meeting with a list of ground rules they alone have developed. Rather, they encourage the team to formulate its own rules of order. Why? When members write their own ground rules, the rules are more likely to be observed. There is buy-in to the rules. Members who don't follow them are likely to feel group displeasure, which for many is worse punishment than criticism by the team leader.

Here are some sample ground rules:

- All meetings will begin and end on schedule.
- The position of chair will be rotated.
- Discussion time will be limited to that set on the agenda.
- Meetings will be held every second Tuesday, from nine-thirty to eleven, in the conference room.
- A few days before the meeting, members will receive a copy of the agenda and any handouts to read and come prepared for the discussion.
- The focus will be on issues, not personalities.

- Only one member will talk at a time.
- Decisions will be made by consensus.
- The group will evaluate each meeting to determine progress toward its objective and the quality of the meeting itself.

Rules mean nothing if they aren't followed. When they aren't, a high-value manager may interrupt the meeting to remind a member of the team's operating guidelines or provide one-on-one counseling after the session if that is more appropriate. But he or she also prevents rule violations from occurring by the management of meetings. For instance, if you set a policy that all meetings will start on time, you need to start all meetings on time—not wait for late arrivals. And to be sure you end on schedule, you and the team need to prepare your agenda so it includes how much time will be allocated to each item. To make sure discussion doesn't continue beyond the time determined, you might want to select someone on the team to act as timekeeper. This person would interrupt to remind the team of its planned agenda. The group then can choose to pick up on this subject at the next meeting or continue on the current subject and postpone another agenda item for the next meeting. This gives you better control of the meeting time.

To make sure members don't forget about an upcoming meeting, you might want to ask someone to send out a reminder note, with the time and location, plus agenda. If guests are expected, they should be identified. (If you want to help members keep track of team progress, you might want to provide room on the back of the agenda sheet for people to take notes and indicate assignments, plus provide a binder in which members can keep their agendas and notes through the life of the project.)

41. Know When and How to Intervene

As leader, you will be serving in the beginning as visionary, helping to set the team's direction, and later as champion, working to make the vision a reality. But in between you will be a facilitator, helping to make the discussion run smoothly, occasionally identifying and remedying team behavior that is impeding the team's performance. You will be monitoring the content of the team—the work being done—but equally important you will be observing the process, that is, how people on the team are working together.

You want to create an atmosphere in which all members of the team feel safe to participate in the discussion.

A high-value manager will welcome all ideas, clarifying poorly worded ideas for the benefit of the group. When someone gets off track, the successful team leader prevents discussions of irrelevant comments without discouraging the member who made the remarks.

You want to get participation from all, which means building the confidence of more-quiet members while discouraging domination by others. You also want to be sure that members talk one at a time, not jumping in before a colleague has finished speaking.

Let's look at some specific problem situations and what you should do:

- *Coping with the silence.* You've asked for ideas or suggestions, and no one speaks up. Maybe the members are unsure how their remarks will be treated. Then you might want to ask one of your more confident team members his or her opinion. This may encourage other members to share their ideas. If this doesn't work, you might try asking members if they have experienced similar or related situations in their careers and how they resolved them.

- *Dealing with complaints about too much work, too little time.* Maybe only one member complains that the team is taking up too much work time. But more members may be feeling the time pressures from participation, so, rather than ignore the one speaker, you might want to relay the question to the group as a whole and ask everyone for alternative options for handling either the project or elements of it.

- *Dealing with a demand to "vote now."* The member who says "Let's get to the vote" wants to save time and insists that further discussion is unnecessary and that it is time to make a decision. First, address the group as a whole to be sure that everyone agrees. You might want the person calling for a vote to spell out the conclusion he or she sees. Then the group can be asked if it agrees or if it would prefer to continue the discussion, maybe just to fine-tune the member's plans.

- *Routing the attacker.* One member disagrees with another's idea, even says, "Tim, I never knew just how limited your thinking was until now." The meeting isn't the place to call the person to task for violating a team ground rule—mixing personalities with ideas. Wait until after the session for a heart to heart. At the meeting, announce to the group as a whole, "I'd like to hear Tim out." Or remind the speaker not to prejudge.

- *Dealing with corporate politics.* If a member attributes another member's comments to an issue of turf or some other questionable motive, you might say to the person, "We're interested in what Sam has to say, not in why he is saying it."

Let's say that you see some violent reaction to a person's idea or comments as attributable to a political motive. Further, you suspect the rest of the group agrees. Under such circumstances, it doesn't pay to ignore the remark. You might want to ask the person outright if he or she might be defensive. Or you might want to use a trick from one group we know that uses a toy duck and the laughter it produces to defuse defensive behavior at its planning sessions. Those who get defensive over statements are passed the "defensive duck."

Along the same lines, another group has a stuffed toy resembling a cow and the "sacred cow" is passed to group members who exhibit signs of trying to keep certain topics untouchable because they are politically sensitive.

• *Eliminating misunderstandings among members.* If misunderstandings are frequent, then they may be attributable to a listening problem. Whether it is one individual or the group as a whole, you might want to suggest that Human Resources put together a training program in active listening for the group. Summarizing in your own words ideas or comments at regular intervals during meetings may also identify areas of confusion.

• *Shutting up excessive talkers.* You might have a member who rambles once he or she has the floor. Or one who just talks and talks and talks. Maybe the person is very enthusiastic about his or her ideas, or maybe he or she is just too talkative. To regain control, wait until the person pauses for breath, then say, "That's an interesting point. Now let's hear from another member of the group." If the person has rambled far afield from the discussion, and has large lungs able to go on forever, it's best to interrupt and alert the person to the fact that he or she is getting off the discussion.

• *Putting an end to side chatter.* Sometimes it seems there is more than one meeting going on. If so, pause. Sometimes the silence for a moment puts an end to the other conversation. If that doesn't work, try calling on one of the talkers to comment on the previous statement. If you need to get tough, you might call the individuals by name, then comment that you need their attention.

• *Getting a positive response from the constant naysayer.* If an individual always disagrees with a decision or comment, you might want to use peer pressure to make this member a better team player. When the naysayer next objects, ask him or her why, then ask the rest of the group to comment. Continuous negativism demands a one-on-one meeting outside the meeting room.

- *Getting the quiet follower to speak up.* You want to draw this person out, but you don't want to make him or her uncomfortable in the process. So you might wait until the person ventures an opinion, then provide positive reinforcement. Next time, ask the person to comment on another's remarks rather than asking for an idea. Follow up with praise. Once you think the person is comfortable with the group, draw him or her out more by asking directly for some suggestion.

- *Taking a stand.* Let's assume that the group has touched on an issue important to you and you want to comment. As leader, you have a position of power that could easily influence the group. So you might want to ask another member of the team to lead the discussion at this point while you participate as a team member.

In using these facilitation techniques, experience is key. The more meetings you lead, the more comfortable you will be in a facilitating role. One bit of advice: You might want to arrive early to meetings and spend time visiting with the members to learn their positions on agenda items. This will prepare you to intervene before confrontations occur or better control them when they do.

As team leader, you really won't be able to take a breather until the project is completed. But a successful conclusion of one project usually means assignment to head up another project. So you may want to measure your leadership of the team. You may want to ask team members the questions below or rate yourself and the team effort. On a scale of 1 to 5 with 1 representing "true," 2 "almost always true," 3 "sometimes true," 4 "often not true" and 5 "never true," how would you rate the following statements:

I had the respect of all the members of my team throughout the project.
$$1 \quad 2 \quad 3 \quad 4 \quad 5$$
The team had a clear goal to work toward.   1   2   3   4   5
I not only called for a commitment from members of the team but demonstrated continually my own commitment to the project as well.
$$1 \quad 2 \quad 3 \quad 4 \quad 5$$
I maintained a flexible leadership style throughout the project, adapting my management style to the circumstances and needs of team members.
$$1 \quad 2 \quad 3 \quad 4 \quad 5$$
I exhibited strong oral and listening skills.   1   2   3   4   5

I put an end to unpleasant situations between team members as quickly as they cropped up.   1   2   3   4   5

I kept personality conflicts from interfering with the team's purpose.   1   2   3   4   5

I did not dominate the meeting or use my position as leader to push through my own ideas.   1   2   3   4   5

Disagreements between members focused on the mission, not personalities.   1   2   3   4   5

Members did not have to shout to get the attention of their peers; members didn't interrupt or show lack of respect to one another.   1   2   3   4   5

At the end of the meeting sessions, members were clear about the conclusions reached.   1   2   3   4   5

When disagreements occurred, either I or another member stepped in to help the disputants reach an accord.   1   2   3   4   5

Members' ideas and suggestions received respectful attention from the group.   1   2   3   4   5

The agendas were realistic, listing just enough subjects to be handled during the session.   1   2   3   4   5

A 1 on each statement, for true, suggests that the team experience was a positive one for you and the team members. While the final measure of a team's success is the answer to the question, Did the team accomplish its mission?, responses to the statements above likely determine the answer to that question.

11

Conflicts Within and Outside the Team

As a high-value manager leading a team, you may find that some disagreements between members can turn into downright conflicts, beyond simple resolution on your part. Sometimes, a member brings to the meetings a history of past grievances with another member that makes that member sensitive to a remark from the other, whether the comment was intentionally hostile or not. Other times, one member's transgression into another member's territory—real or imagined—can cause hostility between the two to the point where members take sides. Attention of the group is no longer focused on the team's mission; rather it is on the situation between the fellow members.

There is the possibility, too, of a conflict arising between you and a member or even a faction of the team because of a view you hold, your openness or lack of openness to ideas, suspicions of favoritism, or what have you.

When any of these situations lead to problems within the group, as a high-value manager you need to be able to:

42. Tolerate those problems that may be making everyone uncomfortable but are also creating more-productive discussions that might generate a better final team outcome.

43. Differentiate between task-oriented and people-oriented conflicts since your response to each type is different.

44. Steer conflicts away from personalities and toward issues.

45. Be aware of those individuals within the team who are most likely to create conflict and help them to work with you, not against you, for the benefit of the team effort.

46. Understand how proxemics can be applied in team situations to defuse conflicts.

47. Know when a conflict is impeding the team's performance and intervention is called for. Sometimes you can smooth things over during the meeting—but not always. When the team is immobilized, then a break may need to be called while you discuss the situation with the combatants outside the room.

48. Mediate a conflict between two team members.

49. Meet one-on-one with individual team members who disagree with your leadership or viewpoint to prevent the differences from impeding the team effort.

50. Overcome concerns of members that their ideas won't get a fair hearing when meetings get intense.

When conflicts arise, it may not be comforting to know that they are more likely to occur in potentially successful teams than in those likely to generate modest results or end in outright failure. But that is true. This is because successful teams are those composed of individuals with different interests and backgrounds that predispose them to disagreements. Further, at meetings these individuals are forever opening the doors to change, a tendency that is also conducive to initiating conflicts.

42. Tolerate Productive Conflicts

Conflict, though stressful, can be more a benefit than a liability if it is channeled to increase members' understanding of one another and, with these new perspectives, to increase group creativity. As members disagree with one another, more ideas than at first come out of the discussion, increasing team productivity. Seeing that conflict is focused in this positive way is a team leader's responsibility.

43. Understanding the Nature of the Conflict

Toward managing conflict to improve team effectiveness, you need to understand the nature of conflicts. They generally fall into two categories: task oriented and people oriented.

Task-oriented conflicts focus on the substance of the work to be done. For instance, conflicts might arise over those who want to get the team task done quickly and those who prefer to proceed more cautiously, or between those who want to rely on previous approaches to resolving the problem and those who want to identify and pursue new methodologies, or between members who believe they can move immediately to brainstorming and others who think they need to fully understand the problem the team is facing. Disagreements may also come about over the final decision, but team ground rules about decision making by consensus can deter different viewpoints from developing into personality conflicts.

People-oriented conflicts are the ones we normally think about when we consider conflicts that arise out of team situations—personality conflicts, struggles for leadership, transgressions into another's operating territory or turf, attempts to increase one's power base at the expense of another team member, and just plain insulting remarks about another's ideas that remain unforgiven and unforgotten.

Let's look at some of the conflicts that can arise during a team effort. Which of these conflicts are task oriented and which are people oriented?

1. Laura would like to conduct further research before reinventing her product, but the team agrees that the time has passed for more research. The consensus is that sufficient research has been done and a decision must be made based on a "leap of faith."
2. Pete interrupts and says, "Jan's ideas never work. I see no point in spending time hearing another from her."
3. Marketing submits as "approved" a list of marketing ideas without discussing its plans with those responsible for the products involved.
4. The group is brainstorming some solutions to an operational problem. Larry has volunteered to write them on the flip chart, but as he writes each one down the group can hear his mutterings—"That's an *A* for sure," "I'd give that an *F*," "Another *D* for Dave."
5. Mark's idea gets shot down. He becomes emotional and leaves the meeting. As the members leave, Dot says to Harriet, "That Mark is a real crybaby. We all have had ideas turned down at some time." Mark overhears the remark and asks to be removed from the task force.

Situation 1 is task oriented: Laura wants more time to reach a conclusion while the rest of the group believes there is no time left. On the other hand situation 2 is clearly people oriented, with a clear conflict in the making between Jan and Pete. Situation 3 really could fall into either category. Marketing seems to think it doesn't have to consult Product Management, whereas Product Management disagrees—on one level, a task-oriented conflict. However, failure to resolve this conflict could lead to a real turf battle between the two operating areas to the ultimate disadvantage of the division or company as a whole.

Situation 4 is more task than people oriented, although Larry's remark about Dave could lead to a personality conflict between the two managers later on. But for now, Larry just doesn't seem to understand that in brainstorming, ideas should not be evaluated until all of them are on paper. Unlike situation 4, situation 5 is more people than task oriented. None of us can say that we aren't hurt when our ideas are turned down. On the other hand, decisions on a team are usually made by consensus. Even if you think your idea is the greatest since sliced bread, your colleagues have the right to choose another idea because they think it is the greatest since bagels.

44. Steer Conflicts Away From People Toward Issues

How should the kinds of problems we've just discussed be resolved? To see, let's look at another team effort:

A Case of Conflict Resolution

Sarah was director of five cold-cereal products for a major food producer. Because there was limited growth potential with the current line of product, senior management had charged Sarah and her group with the task of coming up with a new product, one that might be suitable for new-age cereal eaters. From the first, the product managers wanted to get down to brainstorming ideas for new products, even to selecting new-product names, using current information, whereas the marketing group argued for market research that might determine a viable market niche. The manufacturers felt that whatever new product emerged should fit within the current equipment and material specifications, whereas Sarah and Marketing felt that that issue could not be resolved until the group had come up with a saleable product.

As the group got down to work, problems arose from the first day as the group wrote its mission statement. Dale and Marge, the two product managers, worried about the time marketing's research would take. They faced the possibility of downsizing if there was no immediate action taken. Manufacturing's representatives saw the earlier meetings as a waste of time. "Let us know what you decide, and we'll let you know what it will cost to make," Larry told the team. "Until then, you really don't need us here." He and his two technicians stood up, ready to leave the meeting.

Fortunately, the group had already set ground rules so Sarah was able to stop the defection and disagreement with the *T* (time-out) hand signal. With the group's attention, she then rightfully began on a positive note by asking them, "Can we agree that we want to find a product that will relate to the current health craze?" The members nodded. "Further, can we agree that we are not in a financial position this year to make a mistake?" Again, the members nodded. Then, looking toward Marge and Dale, she continued, "We appreciate your concern about your group. At today's meeting, we will try to identify marketing techniques that will give us the information about the marketplace we need as quickly as possible. Your input at this stage can be very helpful if you know anything about this market." Then, looking at Larry, "I know your time is valuable. But we do need a representative from Manufacturing for all the meetings since it won't help us to come up with a product that we can't manufacture either using our existing equipment or at a cost that will give us sufficient return. If you and your reps can't all attend, can you select one person to represent your group at the meeting?"

"I guess I hadn't seen it from that perspective," Larry said. "Maybe it is better that I attend and send my staff back to work."

Sarah was able to resolve the task-oriented conflict by:

- *Remaining calm.* Since she had mapped out the team's agenda, she likely felt defensive when it was cavalierly dismissed by two thirds of the group. But she stayed calm and did not assert her position of authority.

- *Focusing on the issues.* Sarah then handled the problem by focusing on the issues. The conflict here was on how to proceed, but it easily could have erupted into a conflict among the three groups. Sarah was able to prevent that by focusing on the mission and issues involved.

- *Maintaining communication channels.* It's likely no side was listening to the other, so Sarah had to serve as interpreter, getting the different viewpoints up front before the entire group to help it understand why the team should pursue its objectives as she and the marketing group proposed.

- *Emphasizing mutual interests.* In her comments to the group, she repeatedly returned to the team's mission, the need for the participation of everyone, and the project's impact on the bottom line.

45. Know the Conflict Creators Within Your Team

Sarah was home free but only for a while because as the group began to study the market research, another conflict arose—this one between Dale and the whole group.

The Case of a Conflict Creator

Dale had heard rumors that it was her group that would be downsized, no matter what product was decided on, so she had a chip on her shoulder from the first session of the group. Out of concern, she commenced from day one to try to focus the group's attention on an idea that would benefit her endangered team. As the group discussed survey results, Dale sat smugly, telling the group, "I don't care what the figures show; my idea is best." Tension was growing, and the situation reached a head when Dale brought into the meeting a written proposal for a product, including financials on the cost of producing and marketing the cereal. Sarah saw the potential for a personality conflict arising as Dale's voice became shriller, arguing for her idea against Marge, the other product manager with a downsizing sword over her head, and the marketing group that was still analyzing the survey data.

Once again, by using the signal, *T,* Sarah was able to quiet the members. She thanked Dale for the work she had done, then continued, "We appreciate your concern about your product line. Marge," Sarah's eyes moved from Dale to Marge, "also has concerns about her group. Dale, we will want to consider this product idea of yours, but we need to get to the point where we can make a reasoned decision about any product. In the past, we have moved too quickly." Then, looking at the group as a whole, she asked, "Do you all agree?" With the exception of Dale, the members murmured yes. "Dale," Sarah asked, "can you live with this decision?"

Sarah was able to defuse another conflict by:

- *Emphasizing mutual interests.* While calling for Dale's support and cooperation, she backed up her approach by evoking a little peer pressure from the team. Dale, defensive about her position within the organization, clearly was impatient about getting feedback on her idea, but she agreed to wait to have her idea considered.

Sarah's quick action also sent a message to those members of the group who might have been intimidated by Dale's aggressive stand that, under Sarah's leadership, all viewpoints would be heard and that Sarah would not allow one person to dominate the meeting.

46. Apply Proxemics to Defuse a Situation

Sarah also might have applied proxemics in coping with Dale's outburst. Known to professional trainers, proxemics takes advantage of vertical and horizontal space, room setup, and group dynamics to enable the person in charge of a meeting to better control it. To understand how proxemics works, you only have to consider your childhood school days when your teacher sat at the front of the room behind a desk. That setup sent a message to you and your classmates that the teacher was in charge—and since then you are programmed to consider the person at the front of the room to be the person in control.

Standing up when the others are sitting is also a symbol of control. So Sarah could have stood up as she used the *T* signal to quiet the group. Then she could have used another technique associated with proxemics, moving toward Dale while asking a question in a nondefensive manner designed to get more insights into the nature of the conflict between Dale and the group. She could have said, "Dale, do you think we have reached a point where we can discuss product ideas?" If Dale had said yes, Sarah could have asked why, then questioned that assumption, until she had reached a point where Dale would have realized putting her idea on the table was premature.

Sarah could also have used proxemics to control another of Dale's bad team-meeting habits, assuming she could use place cards at the group table.

Among the participants at that first session was a friend of Dale's, from Manufacturing. During the session, Dale and her pal grinned at each other and smirked when others spoke, sending an unspoken message to their colleagues that they had little respect for them or their ideas. Fortunately, Dale's buddy didn't continue to attend meetings after that first session, but had she, Sarah could have prevented repetition of the situation by placing the two so they couldn't achieve eye contact.

Place cards would also have allowed Sarah to control some of the early tiffs between Marge and Dale by placing Dale beside her. Sarah's nearby presence might have controlled some of Dale's errant behavior.

47. Identify a Conflict Requiring Intervention

Sarah was a good leader who clearly understood her team members. She knew Dale to be high-strung and overprotective of her staff and her turf. So it didn't surprise her that over the next few meetings Dale remained querulous and abrasive.

Intervention Is Called For

> Dale's behavior was counterproductive to the team. She continuously questioned Marketing's assumptions and findings. She told Larry at one meeting that he knew how to make cereal, not what cereal to make so his opinion didn't count, and then proceeded to ignore Larry's remarks throughout the meeting. But her behavior toward Marge was the worst. Any idea from Marge was seen by Dale as a criticism of her operation. She always interrupted Marge, made faces to show her disdain of Marge's ideas, and countered every new suggestion with the idea she had presented originally.

Clearly intervention was called for. In this instance, Sarah actually tolerated the situation too long. Intervention is needed when:

- *Team progress is affected by conflict.* Note that it can be task-related, as well as people-related, conflict. If you have a plan in place, with steps allocated, measuring progress against that timetable will show if the team's effort is being hampered by conflict that demands more than routine measures.
- *Team member contributions decline.* Conflict discourages interest in the project, and the consequence is less creative thinking and less involve-

ment of members in discussions. Listen to the flow of talk. Long periods of silence, particularly of otherwise dynamic contributors, suggest enough of a problem to require intervention. If outspoken members are reluctant to enter the *arena,* or *battleground,* which is what team meetings have become, imagine the impact on your quieter participants who may need prodding to contribute.

▪ *Attendance declines and members who showed enthusiasm early on don't complete their assignments.* Members don't want to go to a meeting where all they will hear is criticism of their thinking or another member's. No one eagerly attends a meeting in which they know they will feel uncomfortable. Rather, they will look for excuses not to attend—a sudden visitor, a phone call, anything to get out of the meeting.

Likewise, assignments no longer become challenging if you expect your efforts will be ridiculed by a fellow member of the team.

In Sarah's case, some of these symptoms were already evident. And a discussion with Dale was long overdue. No one likes to confront someone about her behavior, but when Larry threatened once again to leave the group after a meeting, Sarah knew that she had to intervene. Unfortunately the conflict had grown to the point where it extended outside the meeting room.

A Quarrel in the Corridor

Marge and Dale had picked up a fight begun in the meeting room outside in the corridor. Marge had had an idea for a premium to go into the cereal box, and the group—with the exception of Dale—had been enthusiastic. On the way to their respective offices, Dale had suggested that Marge was using her friendship with one of the marketing team members to get the new product for her team. Marge had finally lost her cool, turned on Dale, and began to upbraid her for her behavior over the last month and a half.

Sarah tried to put an end to the argument, which was becoming louder and more intense, only to be drawn into the fracas herself, when Dale looked at her and said, "You have never supported my ideas. I think the team will once again come up with a loser with you in charge."

Sarah's first goal is to stop the disruption in order to return the workplace to normal as quickly as possible. But sending Dale and Marge back to their offices is only a short-term solution. Clearly, this conflict has to be resolved—and the time has passed when it can be resolved during a meeting. Dale needs to be counseled about her behavior within the team environment (this will be discussed in greater detail in Chapter 12). But there also is a need to mediate the argument between Dale and Marge, since it goes beyond the team discussion to past problems between the two product managers. There is also a personality conflict developing between Sarah and Dale that needs to be stopped before it affects Dale's productivity outside the meeting room, as well as inside. Because any mediation process demands that the mediator be impartial and perceived as such, Sarah may need to call on someone else, like Howard, head of Human Resources, to conduct the mediation.

48. Mediate a Conflict: The Five Steps to Conflict Resolution

Conflict resolution is a five-step process:

Step 1: Identify the source of the conflict. The more information about the cause of the conflict, the more easily it can be resolved. To get the information he will need, Howard can use a series of questions to give him an idea of the cause of the problem, like "When did you first feel upset?" "Do you see a relationship between that and this incident?" "How did this incident begin?"

When you are a mediator, you want to give both parties to the conflict the chance to share their side of the story. It will give you a better understanding of the situation, as well as demonstrate your impartiality. As you listen to each disputant, say, "I see" or "Uh huh," to acknowledge the information as well as encourage them to continue to open up to you.

Step 2: Look beyond the incident. Often it is not the situation but the perspective on the situation that causes anger to fester and that ultimately leads to a shouting match or other visible—and disruptive—evidence of a conflict.

The source of the conflict may be a minor problem that occurred months before, but the level of stress has grown to the point where the two parties have begun attacking each other personally instead of addressing the real problem. In the calm of your office, you can get them to look beyond the triggering incident to see the real cause. Once again, probing questions will help, like "What do you think happened here?" Or "When do you think a problem between you first arose?"

Step 3: Request solutions. After getting each party's viewpoint on the conflict, the next step is to get each to identify how the situation could be changed. Again, question the parties to solicit their ideas. "How can you make things better between you both?"

As mediator, you have to be an active listener, aware of every verbal nuance, as well as a good reader of body language.

Just listen. You want to get the disputants to stop fighting and start cooperating, and that means steering the discussion away from finger-pointing and toward ways of resolving the conflict.

Step 4: Identify solutions both disputants can support. You are listening for the most acceptable course of action. Point to ideas' merits, not only from each other's perspective but in terms of the benefits to the organization. (For instance, Howard might point to the need for greater co-operation and collaboration to effectively address team issues and departmental problems.)

Step 5: Agreement. The mediator needs to get the two parties to shake hands and agree to one of the alternatives identified in step 4. Some mediators go so far as to write up a contract in which actions and time frames are specified. But it may be sufficient to meet with the individuals and have them answer these questions: "What action plans will you both put in place to prevent conflicts from arising in the future?" "What will you do if problems arise in the future?"

This mediation process works as well between groups as it does with individuals. In the case of Dale and Marge, Marge may have been quiet about the barbs from Dale while silently seething. Dale, in turn, may need to voice her fear about favoritism in assigning the new cereal product. But both need to acknowledge each other's expertise and how much more productive they might be if there was greater camaraderie between them—and maybe their staffs. As a first step, they might want to set up monthly meetings of their staffs to share information, insights, and ideas.

49. Address Personality Conflicts/ Leadership Battles With Members, One-on-One Conflict Between You and a Member

Sarah may want Howard to be there when she and Dale discuss the personality conflict that seems to be growing between her and Dale. The mediation process would be very similar to that between Dale and Marge. Or Sarah may want to sit down with Dale to discuss her accusation and clear the air about any rumors or other misconceptions Dale may have about the team's objective.

Most important, Sarah should not lose her temper or allow her frustration with Dale over the past six weeks in team meetings to show. While she might want to point to how cooperative Marge has been, even though a downsizing sword also hangs over her group's head, Sarah is better stressing the common problem the department shares. Sarah might want to defend her past decisions, given Dale's accusation that Sarah's poor leadership is responsible for the division's problems, but the goal of any meeting between her and Dale should be to move toward a better work relationship, not demonstrate who was right and who was wrong. Sarah's objective should be to move away from personality and the past and toward the problem the division now faces and finding a solution.

Sarah might also use questions, as Howard did, to draw Dale out and get her to think about her attitude and its effect on team performance. At the same time, Sarah should consider what influence her supervisory behavior has had on Dale to trigger the complaint. Asking Dale to explain the situation from her viewpoint may reveal some aspects of Sarah's leadership style—perhaps, some unconscious favoritism—that needs to be addressed.

The process is comparable to that in mediation:

1. *Try to understand the other person's views.* You need to hear out the other party. Ask why he or she thinks that way. Even paraphrase what is said to be sure you understand. (Note that understanding doesn't mean that you agree.)

2. *Look for a basis of agreement.* You may not agree with the other person's viewpoint, but you need to find some starting point for discussion. The basis for agreement may be the fact that the other person is upset with your behavior. While acknowledging that, though, don't open the door to a history lesson about all past grievances. Focus on the one incident. In Sarah's case, it is Dale's charge that she is showing favoritism to Marge at team meetings.

3. *Seek solutions.* You want to show that you aim to resolve the difference. So you now want to shift the attention away from the problem toward some solution that is acceptable to both of you. In Sarah's case, it may be a promise to Dale that her idea will get the full attention of the group. On Dale's part, she has to agree to be patient, to participate more

positively in the discussions, weigh her proposal against research data, and be prepared to adapt it if she wants it to get accepted. Further, she has to realize that the final decision about which group gets the project will not be made based on team participation or whose idea is accepted but on a variety of factors, from dollars invested to current staff strengths, to market expertise.

4. *Reach an accord.* Once a compromise has been determined, both parties—in this case, not just Dale but Sarah as well—have to acknowledge acceptance of the compromise. Sarah may have to admit that some of her decisions may have seemed favorable to Marge and that she will be more conscious of her behavior in the future. And Dale will have to promise patience. To be sure that the two understand each other, it might be wise for each to paraphrase what the other has said.

50. **Guarantee a Fair Hearing**

Dale's attitude is somewhat understandable. We all like to believe that our ideas are good, and we want to believe that they will get a fair hearing. In some team situations, enthusiasm runs so high that members begin to try to outshout each other. In such an environment, no matter how fair a manager may be to others' ideas, misperceptions about having their idea shot down before it was voiced can grow.

What can the high-value manager do? As a team leader, you can demonstrate by your own behavior that those with opinions that differ from your own will be heard out. Don't interrupt. Listen respectfully. If you want to voice disagreement, you may want to ask another member to take over the role of chair while you give your viewpoint to the group. You don't allow your leadership position to let you dominate either the discussion or decision making.

Likewise, you don't allow another member to dominate the group. You hear the person out, then ask for other comments or ideas until the group appears to have sufficient ideas from which to choose the best.

Neither should meetings be run so that any member is worried about expressing an idea or an opinion because it might lead to a confrontation with another member. Members feel reassured if they see you actively soliciting ideas and suggestions *you* know might be unpopular with the majority of the group. When an outspoken member interrupts another and puts down that member's idea, and you say, "I want to hear Sally out. I won't know if I disagree or not until I understand why she believes as she does," know that the group is applauding you, albeit silently, for making it clear that all opinions will get heard. Not only will your actions encourage those with divergent ideas to speak up but they will likely help your team reach a better conclusion or result. A lot of teams begin with the assumption that they will identify the perfect idea—the Holy Grail of ideas—only to discover that the best idea is one that is hammered out in good-natured conflict from bits and pieces of everyone's ideas.

12

How to Coach/How to Counsel in Team Settings

Some team members will require little direction and encouragement, while others may need not only coaching but some counseling to get them to pull their weight throughout the team process.

The coaching might entail some training in problem-sensing or -solving skills, or some refocusing of attention on the team's mission when the group loses sight of its objectives, or praise and recognition for tasks well done.

But there may also be specific performance problems that call for the team leader to counsel a member or group of members. It may be a matter of an overdue team assignment that is causing the team to fall behind its schedule, or it could be a member who continually arrives late for meetings, disrupting the discussions. Then the team leader has to be more than a facilitator or coach—then he or she, as counselor, has to work with the problem team member to get that person to fulfill his or her responsibilities to the group.

The roles of coach and counselor call for a high-value manager who knows how to:

51. Coach for enthusiasm and high performance.

52. Overcome organizational roadblocks to achievement of the team's mission.

53. Oversee training where needed.

54. Use peer pressure to help reform a non–team player or get work associated with the team effort done. If the team has an informal leader, for example, you have to know how to use this person's influence for the benefit of the group as a whole.

55. Meet and discuss performance problems with members who aren't pulling their weight, even managers who aren't your direct report,

without alienating them or undermining the rapport among team members.

51. Coach for Enthusiasm and High Performance

When individuals first get together as a team, they are eager to participate. This level of interest can last a long time or it can be relatively short-lived. Team participation can take up considerable time, and members may need a reason to exert the extra energy that involvement in a high-performance team requires.

As coach, you need to give them that reason by:

• *Providing praise and positive feedback to team members.* Letting members know that their contribution to the effort is appreciated will encourage them to continue to contribute at a high level to the team.

The value of praise has been extolled in almost every management textbook, but praise continues to be rarely given when deserved in traditional manager-employee relationships, let alone in team settings where it has equal, if not greater, value since the supervisor/subordinate work relationship is often missing. When a member contributes significantly to the team, be ready to give praise. Point out the impact of the achievement on the team's mission. If the team member has been quiet during past meetings due to insecurity, use the accomplishment to give the person the self-confidence he or she needs to take a more vocal role in the group as well as take on tougher team assignments.

• *Making sure that responsibilities are clear.* Confusion can add to the stress of team participation. So when tasks are delegated to team members, the assignments need to be given with the same specificity that one would use when delegating to an employee. That is, members need to know why the task must be done, when the work is to be completed and how rigid that deadline is, how the finished work will be measured, how important the task is in relation to the other work being done, and how the task fits into the bigger picture of the team's mission.

• *Anticipating problems before they occur, identifying solutions to resolve them when they do occur, and setting up procedures to prevent them from occurring again.* For instance, a team leader who learned that one of the team's members had had to travel suddenly on business and could not complete a team assignment on schedule, would immediately reassign that task to another to be sure that the travel plans didn't hold up work on the project. Or a member who reported being unable to reach a key source of information might be given the name of another individual who could provide the same information or someone who would help the member reach the first individual. Likewise, a member who uses the term "your" when referring to the project may need to be gently reminded that the right pronoun is "our," even reassured that he or she is, indeed, a key part of the team.

• *Monitoring group progress to be sure that the team effort and mission are still in concert.* Circumstances may necessitate a change in the team's mission. Or decisions made by the team may unconsciously divert the group's efforts from the original mission. In either event, alert the team to the situation. Under your leadership, the group may want to reconsider its activities to be sure that they are correctly focused. Or its members and you may agree to take a new direction in light of the changing situation.

• *Ensuring two-way communication between the team and mentor or senior management.* As team leader, you are the person responsible for seeing that communications occur upward and downward. Earlier, we described how you will be facilitating discussion during meetings to be sure that productive communications occur among members. Equally important is seeing that key developments affecting the team's mission are shared with the members, and that management is alerted to member concerns and any problems encountered. The team's members need to feel that they are "in" on things, while management needs to appreciate any obstacles the team is encountering so it can remove them. Personal problems of team members as well as problems of the team as a whole may have to be communicated if they affect the ability of the team to achieve its mission.

• *Demonstrating your respect for the knowledge, skills, and abilities team members bring to the effort.* You do this by sharing the decision making with the team members; by showing no favoritism when giving assignments—both the drudge chores and the fun tasks are shared equally among team members; by demonstrating that you respect member opinion by truly listening to their views; by empowering team members to manage their own assignments; and by being constructive with your suggestions, not dictatorial.

52. Overcome Organizational Roadblocks

As coach, the team leader may have to overcome organizational roadblocks the team encounters. The roadblock may be a person or a system, policy, or procedure. A system or procedure may exist that complicates the team's ability to get information to achieve its mission. Or even in a project that is good for the entire organization, there may be one individual who sees the effort as a threat, and consequently withholds key information from the team.

As team coach, the high-value manager will approach the human roadblock or redirect the team member to another resource with the same or related information. If it is a policy or system that is blocking the team effort, he or she might consult with the team's mentor or sponsor to see if there is some way around the procedural wall.

53. Oversee Training Where Needed

To complete their group's mission, the team members may need to fine-tune certain skills or develop others, and the team leader, as coach, has to identify these deficiencies, then overcome them.

High-value managers know that certain skills are critical to team effort and will either consult with Human Resources or the appropriate executive to have the team trained in these areas if the team lacks them—as Sal did in the following case study—or conduct the training themselves.

Getting the Needed Training

Sal headed up a group from warehousing that was looking into some problems with shipping. Sal knew that problem-sensing and problem-solving skills would be essential to the team's success, but he also knew that he and members of the team had never undergone any specific training to equip them to identify the cause behind the shipping delays his plant was experiencing.

The group knew that a problem existed but the group was unlikely to do more than attack symptoms without some training in the various techniques that are used in continuous improvement or total quality management—techniques like variance analysis, Pareto charts, and the like. Previous attempts at solving the problem had failed just because the other groups had lacked this skill, and Sal felt his own group would have no better luck unless it received training.

So Sal proposed to the plant manager that the team get

the training it needed. The group would learn how to define a problem, gather information that might cast a new light on the problem, determine likely solutions, then choose the best idea. Since Sal suspected there might be several ideas that would come out of brainstorming after the *real* problem was identified, he also asked that the group be trained in multivoting to reach consensus.

Problem sensing and solving are skills that many teams lack. But there are others as well. Some teams have serious deficiency in interpersonal skills. Others are unskilled in negotiation and consequently have problems getting all the resources they need to accomplish their objective. Still others lack the ability to network within and outside the organization, as Mel's team did.

Training a Team in Networking

Mel's team had been asked to submit a cost-savings plan for inventory control and distribution. But to do that, the group decided it needed to compare its operation to others within the region. But the team members lacked friends in other companies they could contact for information they could use to compare their own operation with.

Fortunately, Mel had worked for two other companies before joining Supply Depot, and he still had good friends there. He was able to ask the two individuals to share their experiences with the group. Mel, in his role as coach, invited his friends to stay for lunch, and during lunch he watched as members of his team asked for the names of other contacts they could call for additional information.

A high-value manager, Mel proved he could be an excellent trainer, teaching networking by doing it at a team meeting and later over meatballs and spaghetti at a local eatery.

After a few sessions, high-value managers should step back from their team effort to identify weaknesses of the group as a whole and of individual members. Whenever possible, training or other support should be given to increase the team's chances for success.

54. Handle Non–Team Players

Whereas coaching is designed to train a group and reinforce positive feelings within a group, counseling primarily deals with problems in individual member performance.

A team's purpose, membership, and culture all influence the amount of counseling you may be called on to do. For instance, members of a team whose success could mean the survival of the company would not need urging to complete assignments on time. With a group in which members hold each other in great respect, peer pressure might resolve any problem with a member that arises, eliminating the need for your intervention. Likewise, a group that has worked together for some time may have an informal leader who can discuss a problem with a colleague over drinks before the situation demands your formal attention.

Where the team operates in a climate of trust, a problem may be surfaced by one of the members and discussed and resolved by the team as a whole—even a problem having to do with one member's contribution.

If the team is made up of staff members, any problems about team participation may be handled as a part of your regular supervisory duties if the team member's participation is also a part of his or her day-to-day job.

Guidelines set during the forming stage of the team can also prevent some situations that would require your intervention, like procedures for decision making that should prevent disagreements over the group's final recommendations or conclusions.

The most sensitive situations requiring counseling will involve teams in which your co-members are your peers. Even if counseling is truly needed, members may resent your intervention. So, needless to say, any steps taken must be done tactfully.

Allow enough time for the group to pressure the non–team player to play by the rules of the team or to find a way to get a harried team member to complete his or her assignments on time. Even create the opportunity for just such team feedback by initiating monthly team-conducted critiques that allow the members to do their own counseling, as well as praising, of member contributions.

To encourage members to complete assignments on time—and prevent a problem with overdue work from ever occurring—try hanging up a chart in the team meeting room that keeps track of team assignments.

A manager with an overdue task need not be spoken to—the chart would speak loudly enough about the individual's failure to hold up his or her part of the team effort. To be sure the message is loud and clear, the chart could be designed to show how completion of one task by a member was essential to another's completion of his or her assignment.

If a member doesn't inform you until a meeting about his or her inability to complete an assignment for that session, if a member spends the time talking about everything and anything but the team subject, if you learn that a member is delegating to other team participants his or her tasks without alerting you, if a member seems vague about his or her responsibility to the team and shows little interest in the team discussion, and if a clique begins to form within the team that makes it more difficult for you to hold productive meetings, then a one-on-one meeting with the problem member is called for, regardless of his or her relationship to you.

55. Discuss Performance Problems

In counseling the member who is not fulfilling his or her responsibilities to the group, your objective is to make clear the effect of continued poor performance on the team's effort and the need for an immediate change in behavior. Earlier we talked about how you would confront someone on the team with whom you have a personality conflict. There are similarities between those sessions and a counseling session. In conflicts with a team member, your objective may be to reach a compromise (including agreeing to disagree), but in counseling a team member your goal has to be to identify the cause of the problem behavior, change that behavior for the good of the team effort, and/or make a decision about a member's continued participation on the team.

Counseling is a six-step process:

1. *Describe the situation.* Refer to facts as you know them. Remember, no matter whom you are counseling—whether peer or staff member—don't be judgmental. Explain that you have to discuss the person's behavior because of the importance of the team effort and the person's potential contribution to it.

2. *Listen.* Give the person a chance to explain what has been happening. To draw the person out, as well as show your colleague (or staff member) that you are willing to listen, use such active listening techniques as paraphrasing what you hear and asking questions. Don't interrupt. Nod your head or say "Uh huh" as the person speaks.

3. *Restate the consequences of a continuation of the situation.* You want to acknowledge the member's explanation, but you also don't want to give him or her license to continue. So, once again, you need to describe the impact on the team mission if the problem continues.

4. *Identify behavioral changes.* You and the team member have to come up with an action plan that will either change the member's behavior or its impact on the team. For instance, a member who is dealing with multiple deadlines might not be able to make a team task deadline but he or she could be given help by another member until the work crisis in his or her regular job disappears.

Experience has shown that those plans suggested by the person being counseled are most likely to be implemented.

5. *Get a commitment for action.* The team member has to accept responsibility for changing his or her behavior in support of the team's mission.

6. *Provide feedback and support.* If you were counseling one of your staff members about his or her regular job performance, you would get together with the individual and plan for regular meetings in which the person's progress would be discussed. With a team member who is also a peer, you might want to offer less formal feedback—a "smile" at a meeting, praise for a job well done, a memo of thanks to be inserted in the person's personnel file.

Failure to change behavior might necessitate another meeting, perhaps to suggest a change in membership and selection of an alternate who can work more effectively or productively with the team.

Where a person's skills are essential but a problem exists, and you and the manager report to the same executive, an informal word to senior management might be in order. Or, perhaps a better tactic, invite a member of senior management to a team meeting to remind the problem performer of the importance of the team's mission.

Throughout this process, don't criticize or moralize. If you do, you will create feelings of animosity toward you that can divert attention from the team's goal.

How does this process work in real life? Let's take the case of a friend of ours, Jeri.

Remotivating a Problem Performer

Jeri heads up public relations. Trudy, one of her staff members, proposed a four-page insert on quality for the company's in-house newsletter. Jeri was so enthusiastic about the idea that she asked Trudy to form a small team to develop a prototype. Later in the day, Jeri shared Trudy's idea with her own boss. He thought the insert was a good idea, but that a better one was an ongoing newsletter for staff distribution on that topic. "It will reinforce senior management's message about TQM," he explained to Jeri.

Jeri thought that Trudy would be delighted about her boss's suggestion, but instead Trudy seemed put out that her vision had taken on a new character. It wasn't a matter of credit. Trudy was the acknowledged originator of the idea, and Jeri had asked Trudy to continue to take ownership of the project—so it wasn't that Trudy's idea was being given to another to implement, either. But as Jeri waited impatiently to see a sample issue, she began to hear rumors about problems within the team.

Trudy was no longer enthusiastic, and her lack of interest was becoming evident to her fellow team members. Tasks that Trudy *owned* were not done on time. Often she delegated to other members of the team responsibilities that she alone had the knowledge and experience to handle. Jeri knew that the problem didn't lie with Trudy's workload—Jeri had transferred some tasks to other PR staff to free Trudy to give the project her full attention.

So Jeri decided to attend a meeting of the team. For someone who was generally so upbeat about her job, Trudy came into the meeting looking downtrodden. Throughout the session, Jeri watched as Trudy perfunctorily answered questions and unenthusiastically moved the group along. Not only was Jeri worried about Trudy's attitude, but she became concerned because two other team members seemed to have caught the condition as well. Jeri didn't want to take over the project—she wanted Trudy to do this on her own since she had hoped that it would justify a long-overdue promotion for Trudy to assistant manager. But Jeri knew she had to do something or the project was doomed.

When Jeri met later with Trudy, a chip on Trudy's shoulder was clearly evident. Jeri reaffirmed the importance of the project to the company and voiced her concern that work was not proceeding as quickly as she had hoped. Trudy didn't hold back. "I'm not sure this newsletter will work. I had some ideas for stories, but they won't work now. I don't know how this product will be received. I wish I had had a chance to explain why the four-page insert was a better approach. Now I feel stuck with something that likely won't work." Then, after a pause, Trudy said, "Whatever happens, I don't want to be associated with this newsletter once it gets started."

Jeri was shocked. She was used to staff's begging to take over new publications, not rejecting a high-visibility project the way Trudy had done. But Jeri now understood Trudy's lack of enthusiasm. Trudy didn't think the idea, as changed, would succeed. And she didn't want to be held accountable for its failure.

Jeri told Trudy, "We all know that print products evolve. Once you have a sample to look at, we will show it to both senior management and some employees. We'll determine if it will contribute to the corporate TQM effort. I think it will work. If it doesn't, it doesn't. All we can expect is that you do the best job you can. You are familiar with the issues to address. You're vital to the project."

Jeri then went on to explain that Trudy's vision had triggered the idea for the newsletter, and that she should be pleased—not upset—about the reaction from management. Further, Jeri explained, no product was solely the result of one person's thinking. The vision is the foundation on which others—to begin with, Trudy's team—would be building their thoughts.

Trudy agreed "to take ownership" of the newsletter, while Jeri offered to sit in on a few more sessions with members from Quality Assurance. This would help the team refine the idea.

Reviewing Jeri's meeting with Trudy, first note that she identified the nature of the problem—Trudy's lackluster behavior (step 1). She pointed up the need for Trudy to role-model a positive attitude for the team and identified behavior on Trudy's part that could create problems for the project, like Trudy's missed deadlines.

Then Jeri listened to Trudy as she told her side of the situation (step 2). Jeri demonstrated her willingness to hear Trudy act by nodding her head, interjecting an occasional "uh huh," and paraphrasing what she heard to be sure that she was clear about the problem. Then Jeri restated the consequences of Trudy's inattention to the project (steps 3 and 4)—not only failure of the project but a poor performance rating at the end of the year.

Jeri then paused to allow the message to be truly understood by Trudy: By not giving the project the attention it should get, she was guaranteeing its failure. Trudy knew she had no other choice but to give the project her best and agreed to do so. Jeri, in turn, assured Trudy that she would provide staff, time, and other resources to help the project succeed. While Trudy would still have ownership of the project, Jeri's presence at the meeting meant that the project had high-priority status, something that would help rebuild the enthusiasm of the other team members (steps 5 and 6).

In this instance, Jeri was the team's mentor, but she assures us that she has used the same six-step process when she has headed teams, and that the procedure works effectively.

Consider your own coaching and counseling skills. Circling 1 for "always," 2 for "almost always," 3 for "sometimes," 4 for "almost never," and 5 for "never," answer the following questions:

When a team member lets the team down, I remain objective about the member being counseled.   1   2   3   4   5
I make clear to team members what is expected of them both individually and as a part of the team.   1   2   3   4   5
I help members have access to the information and people they need to do their team assignments.   1   2   3   4   5
I share decision making with the team members.   1   2   3   4   5
I let those responsible for some part of the team effort decide for themselves how the job will be done.   1   2   3   4   5
I have identified within the team those informal leaders who can help me coach and counsel the other members.   1   2   3   4   5
I make sure that everyone on the team knows who "owns" what assignments.   1   2   3   4   5
I intervene when an attitude problem or other situation is counterproductive to the team's mission.   1   2   3   4   5
I keep the team members informed of developments that might call for a shift in mission or effort.   1   2   3   4   5
I monitor the team effort to see that it is meeting its schedule and is on track.   1   2   3   4   5
I anticipate problems and act to prevent them from occurring.
                                                       1   2   3   4   5

If you can answer "always" to each of these statements, you are doing your job as coach and counselor—and team leader!

13

How to Get What Your Team Needs

In most organizations, resources—money, people, time—are scarce. Even the most successful organization has limited resources, which means difficult decisions have to be made about how resources will be allocated. As a high-value manager, you often will find yourself vying with other departments for funding. As team leader in an organization with several teams under way, each in need of personnel, equipment, and funds, the problem is even greater. There is only so much money and other critical resources that an organization can spend on untested products, services, or solutions to problems. While the long-term costs of not spending are usually significant, most firms wrongly hold back to save money on the short term. Which means that you may need to make a strong case for your team. Or you may have to do a lot of horse trading, a lot of "I'll give you this if you give me that" with other managers to get what your team needs.

Therefore, to help your team achieve its objective, as a high-value manager you need to:

56. Be able to present your team and its goals persuasively.

57. Position requests strategically.

58. Negotiate skillfully—get what you want without making enemies.

59. Be flexible—able to adjust your negotiating strategy to achieve results.

56. Present Your Team and Goals Persuasively

The first, and most likely, source for the resources your team may need to accomplish its mission is the team's sponsor or senior management.

But to make a strong case for people or money, you will need to come up with more than wishful thinking—for example, a business plan for a new product that demands up-front money for market research and test marketing or a cost-benefit analysis of a solution to a problem. Yes, you will need to prove that you can save money or make money if you are to get money to spend.

To be sure that you send the right message when you make a request, the paperwork itself should contain:

- *The objective in the form of a clear statement of the results to be achieved.* This statement may reflect the mission statement the team developed during its first few meetings, with some summary statement about how the team *plans* (a critical word, since management will want evidence that careful thought was given to the request) to achieve its objective.

Besides the goal itself, you may want to offer a persuasive argument for the goal; that is, the "why." When the "why" reflects the strategic direction of your organization, you increase the chances of getting management approval.

- *How you plan to achieve the objectives.* You need to provide detail about how the goal will be accomplished. For instance, if you plan to introduce a new product, then you will want to do market research or develop a prototype to show to a focus group, test market the product, train customer service about the product's use, and so forth. Besides each activity or step in the process, describe the result of the step, perhaps even preparing your proposal so that the result of each activity is presented as a subset of the final goal. This makes the relationship between the goal and each activity doubly clear.

To be sure that you have identified every critical activity, sit down as a team to develop a workflow diagram that takes the project from start-up to completion.

- *Why the funding is needed.* Much of the project may be done with current staff, facilities, and other resources. But there may be a need to purchase either equipment or services. You need to explain this. For instance, if your organization's marketing staff hasn't the time, or the team believes it may get more objective results from doing so, you may want to outsource both market research and the running of focus groups to test the prototype on targeted audience groups.

- *How long the project will take.* Everyone wants a timetable. And no one more than management, since it will want to know when it can expect to get a return on money spent.

To get a clear idea of the time frame in which you will be working, start backwards from goal achievement to present. Don't forget to give yourself some leeway; remember, no matter how dedicated your team members, they have full-time jobs, with day-to-day responsibilities that must be fulfilled, as well as their team assignments. Don't set unrealistic turnaround times in order to convince management to fund your project; it will only put undue pressure on your team. And if you don't make the dates, it will go against future team efforts.

▪ *How much funding is required to complete the work.* In your proposal, you need to include information on both expenditures and return on investment, including projected income or savings over x years assuming you are proposing a new product or service or operational improvement. You will have to show that the money, if spent on your goal, would be more productive than if it were spent elsewhere. There are many textbooks that provide detailed instruction on doing business plans or cost-benefit analyses, but let us just remind you here of the need for conservatism in developing any financials, no matter how enthusiastic your group may be about its idea. Remember, the wise team does better than it has projected, thereby seeming even more successful.

What if the project is not tied directly to either new revenue or savings? Perhaps you are proposing a new customer service system that will minimize customer delivery problems. There is a cost to purchase new equipment but the improvement will be better customer relations, which is not something that lends itself easily to a profit projection. In such a situation, you might point to improved customer relations which, in turn, could promote customer retention. There you might use retention rates or other projections to suggest the worth of your equipment purchase.

In situations where no numbers of any kind can be pointed to in order to demonstrate the worth of a financial outlay, admittedly you will have a harder job of selling your proposal. But then point to softer benefits and hope that management sees the relationship between better employee relations and morale or improved workflow or a less stressful workplace to increased staff productivity.

57. Position Your Request *Strategically*

As we mentioned, you are more likely to get approval from senior management if your objective mirrors a strategic business objective, or if it addresses a problem that currently puts the firm at a disadvantage against competitors. Whatever the reason for your request for funds, it is important to see the request from management's perspective—as an investment from which it will either make money, save money, or increase productivity. If you develop your numbers with that view in mind, you are more likely to get management's approval on your request. Likewise, your own worth will increase as top managers see you share their attitude about spending money to make money. Then take your proposal to that senior officer who can most benefit from your team's efforts—if not your sponsor—to get his or her support. That means that you will have at least one ally, maybe two, including the team's sponsor, when your request is reviewed.

Let's assume that you are proposing a systems improvement for the customer service area. Your organization's objective is to improve its bottom line through new product development plus changes in existing product line. The system you have in mind will bring on screen data about customers that will allow your reps to identify protential purchasers of the new products, information about existing product changes, and the history of customers, including former purchases that they no longer order. With these data on screen, your reps can handle incoming orders, alert customers to changes in product that they walked away from but now might want to reconsider, and tell them about products they might want to purchase that the company has just introduced. This system could help your firm increase market share in several product lines, plus support new product introductions. So you might want to get the support of R&D as well as the person to whom you report, likely the marketing vice president or sales vice president.

58. Negotiate Skillfully

Let's assume that you submitted your request for funds but were turned down. Times are tough, and money is scarce. While management is willing to help fund a portion of the project, you will need to get help from other areas of the organization to complete the team's mission.

You have set up a team of staff members for the purpose of developing an on-line data system that will provide valuable information on your division's customers, information that up to now has not been available to any part of the organization. Management is willing to contract with the firm you identified, and you and your staff have identified your information needs, but you feel you need an expert to work with the outside firm to be sure that the database meets your department's needs. But management has drawn the line about further funding. What should you do?

First, you need to ask yourself, "Is there a department or division within the organization with the resources—people or money—to do the work?" The second question is: "If there is, would it give us the hand we need?"

Remember, resources are scarce. Even if you point to the indirect benefits from successful implementation of your team's project to all within the organization, a colleague may not be willing to help either finance or staff an effort unless the manager sees a direct benefit to his or her operation.

If there is a way to bring the manager into your project, then you are more likely to get his or her cooperation. But if there is no direct benefit from your project, then you may need to do a little horse trading.

Horse trading can be done over coffee or lunch, even standing by the water cooler or, in this day and age, the network printer; it's informal negotiations in which you approach the other manager, then describe your problem, make an offer, and wait to see if the manager agrees or not. It's not always—even ever—a fair exchange. If you are giving something worth one thousand dollars, you may think you should get something worth one thousand dollars back. But a more accurate measurement of a good horse trade is if you get something you want.

Horse traders in the old West knew that the secret to success was having the right credentials (a good horse), a good reputation, and a good sales pitch. In today's terms, that means, first, having a project that has management's support and a good chance of success (the horse should look like a good runner). Second, you yourself need to have a good reputation for keeping promises made to fellow managers—that is, if you offer to send a staff member to lend a hand, you send a staff member to lend a hand; you don't have a reputation for a faulty memory over such offers (you have been a good horse trader in the past). Finally, you know how to make your request. You have done some research, have thought through what you can offer, and have rehearsed your remarks so you can make the other manager think you have something to offer.

Remember, you are going to the other party for help, and right now he or she holds all the cards. So you have to be prepared to do some compromising to get what you and your team need. (Incidentally, the same rules apply to horse trading for any organizational purpose.)

Let's look at our database scenario.

Let's assume that Kevin, who heads up another division of the company, has a staff member, Jim, who in a previous job oversaw setup of a system similar to the one you plan. Jim now has nothing to do with systems development, but he has told you he would be willing to provide the assistance your team needs if he just had the time. Maybe there is a way you can help Jim find the time, assuming Kevin is agreeable, and thereby get Jim's help on the team project.

So you make it a point to bump into Kevin and suggest lunch. But first you do some research to find out what you can "trade" Kevin for Jim's time. What would Kevin's objections be to your request? What's your sales pitch to overcome those objections? Is Kevin in the midst of a project that you can provide help with? Could the outcome of your project possibly favorably affect Kevin's operation? Assuming that Kevin is agreeable, is there anyone on your own staff who can do some of Jim's work? If not, what other options do you have? Would you have to go to a third manager to borrow a Jim fill-in, thereby calling for further horse trading?

Let's assume you discover that Jim's work can be done by one of your staff members, and while Kevin would not benefit from the team project, he might benefit from marketing assistance. You happen to have some friends outside the organization familiar with the targeted market who might spend some free time with Kevin's marketing staff. (If Kevin had had a need for the data your system would collect, the negotiation session could easily have turned into a problem-solving session, with both of you working together to solve the same problem.)

So how do you approach the negotiations so that both you and Kevin come out satisfied?

You have to explain to Kevin the purpose of the team effort. Then you have to explain your need for help from Jim.

You have your bargaining chips—either a staffer to help make up for the time that Jim spends on the team project, or marketing advice and counsel via your outside network. Or you can remind Kevin that being a team player is good for his corporate reputation. (Although it might not be in your best interests to say so, the obverse is equally true: Not being a team player is not good for his reputation.)

Before discussing your idea with Kevin, check with your sponsor or own boss to be sure that he or she will be pleased with whatever deal you strike. And during your meeting with Kevin, communicate to him senior management's support of your team's mission to date. Give him reason to want to get involved.

Kevin is a nice guy who is likely to agree to one of your two offers. But don't take advantage of the situation by doing a power play, bulldozing your way through. Fast talking may get you what you want, but it would at the expense of future cooperation or impairment of your own reputation. (Besides, those who don't think they got a fair deal may come back and renegotiate for higher stakes, even with someone at a higher level at their side to bolster their position.)

Kevin is agreeable to let you have Jim but only for a month, at the start of the project. In return, he wants access to your external network and help in doing Jim's work over a two-month period. At first you are sufficiently annoyed to want to stop negotiations and consider alternatives to getting a systems helper, even go back to consideration of other ways to complete the project without a systems helper. But you can't allow the heat of negotiations to cause you to lose sight of the project's need for a system's expert. Remember, as the person seeking help, you are in the weaker negotiating position. So you accept. You will go along with providing an extra month of help to Kevin and Jim even if you don't think it is fair. The bottom line is you both have won.

Let's look at some key reasons why the negotiations were successful:

1. You were open to changing your position—you agreed to give more to get what you wanted.

2. You listened to what Kevin had to say. He alerted you to a deadline Jim had that could interfere with his helping you unless he had additional assistance, so he offered an alternative solution—which you were agreeable with.

3. You knew your objectives but were flexible about the position you would take. You didn't say, "I need to achieve A; to do that, I will do B and C." Rather, you said, I need to achieve A; help me to figure out what I will need to do to get that."

You tried to understand Kevin's objectives, concentrating on his goals and not his demands, or your own need to outtrade him.

4. You didn't expect Kevin to be concerned about your needs. While you began by explaining your needs, you allowed Kevin to turn the conversation around to discuss his needs and addressed those in order to achieve your own.

5. Neither one of you can be seen as a loser. Kevin had you make a further concession, but in that you both got what you wanted—you both came away with something that will help you—which is the true purpose of good negotiation. Everyone wins, and, in the end, the real winner is your organization.

Issues and facts are important, but it is often the communication style of the negotiator that influences the final outcome. So, besides the issues being negotiated, keep in mind the need to be:

- *Unemotional.* Stay calm, cool, and collected at all times—don't let the give and take of negotiations cause you to overreact.
- *Sincere.* If you are horse trading, the other manager needs to know that he or she can trust you to keep your word.
- *Self-confident.* Old-time horse traders did their homework before negotiations to exude self-confidence.
- *Flexible.* You have to be willing to change your negotiating plan if you want the other person to change his or hers.
- *Congenial.* The best horse traders keep the atmosphere friendly and nonadversarial. The point they want to make is, "By giving me what I need, you will get what you want in turn. How about it?"

59. Be Flexible

In the situation with Kevin, he was amendable to a trade, but not all managers will be at first. Some will be indecisive initially, requiring you to check back, even do some more horse trading before you get a final answer. Which may be yes or may be no.

If you make your offer and it is refused, don't become insistent or threaten. Such response will only create further resistance. Instead, ask questions to clarify the objections.

Is the manager's objection that he doesn't need a horse at all, or is it that he doesn't need a roan or a bay? He wants a pinto. Or you have a sprinter, and she needs a Morgan, a real workhorse. Or right now he can't make a deal—he hasn't the resources to spare—but maybe a month from now circumstances will be different.

Probe to better understand the person's situation. "What is the problem?" "Why can't he do this?" And, most important, ask, "What if we. . . ?", which may reopen the door to negotiation by making the other manager not the solution to the team's dilemma but a part of the problem-solving team.

Go further and ask the person for advice. He or she may have an answer you and your team haven't considered. Maybe this manager can become a horse trader for you if he or she is able to share the glory if the project succeeds.

But the more time you spend with the person you are trying to trade with, the better you will understand his or her needs, and the greater the chance that you will come up with an offer that he or she can't refuse.

But let's say that, no matter what you do offer, the person refuses. While you will be disappointed—maybe, even angry—you need to practice the communication styles we described earlier. You shouldn't let your disappointment about your fellow manager's refusal to go along with your idea sour your longer-term relationship—after all, you don't know all the pressure he or she is under; it could be that the person would like to help but just can't release staff time or resources to you. Then you need to go back to review your contingency plans.

Who else within the organization can you turn to for help? Are there areas within the company with which you are unfamiliar that might have the resources you need? Maybe you need to send out scouts from your team to scour the organizational climate to identify likely opportunities for horse trading. (Keep in mind that you may have animals other than horses to trade; there may be someone who needs a goat or a cow or even corn, and you may have some in your silo.)

Another option: Your own team members may have skills with which you are not familiar. Going back to our case, maybe there is someone with a marketing background or some past experience in market research and focus groups who would be interested in doing the task but feels she doesn't have the time. What do you have to offer her to get her to put in those extra hours? Can one of the other team members lend her a hand with her day-to-day job to free her to do the tasks? Finally, does one of your team members have special influence with the manager who wouldn't horse trade? Is it worth another, tactful try?

Never give up.

In horse trading, you have to maintain a positive attitude. Those you negotiate with will sense your self-confidence, and it will influence how they respond to you—and your team's needs.

To measure how successful a horse trader you are, answer the questions below with a yes or a no.

- Do you tend to make large concessions?
- Are you so frightened about reaching a stalemate, that you agree to a position just to end negotiations?
- Do people complain that you demand too much?
- Do you threaten when you don't get your way?
- Are you more concerned about retaining your current relationship, at the expense of the negotiation?

These questions reflect the two extremes in negotiation. To be a successful negotiator—and horse trader—you need to take the middle ground:

- *Be adaptable.* If an alternative offer will get you what you want, and the alternative does not mean sacrificing something dear to you, then give it serious consideration. Don't make the negotiation into a power game—you may win the battle but lose the war.
- *Take inventory.* Know how far you can bend without breaking.
- *Study the other person's needs.* Find out the individual's objectives, needs, and resources. Maybe you have some common interests, which will allow you to work together, rather than horse-trade, to solve the problem.
- *Know what not to ask for.* There may be some things you want but someone else has to have for the good of the overall organization. Don't fight over it or hold a grudge. Give in with good grace.
- *Involve everyone in your success.* If the project is a success, don't you and your team hog the glory; share it with those managers who helped, whether freely or through horse trading. It will add to your reputation as a fair and honest horse trader.

14

Maintaining Team Momentum as You Reach Your Goal

In the role of team leaders, high-value managers must know how to motivate—even know how to sell—members and others on the importance of the team's mission. This ability is essential throughout the team process but becomes especially important as the team concludes its work and submits its recommendations to the team's sponsor or management for approval.

As you start the team process, you need to interest and challenge potential members sufficiently so they want to be a part of the team. Later, as the team encounters obstacles in its way, you need to convince your members that the effort they are putting into the project is worthwhile. But, even more important, you may have to convince other managers within your organization of the benefits to them of helping the team over those obstacles, perhaps even talking them into providing additional funds, staff, information, or other resources. No easy task!

During the norming or performing stage of the team process, if the team is sponsored by a member of top management, you may have to have him or her intervene, too, to remove political obstacles in the path of the team. Finally, upon completion of the project, you may need to sell the team's conclusions to management as a whole, not just the team's sponsor or the head of the division that the team's effort is to help.

As a part of your ongoing leadership job, you will need to:

60. Keep the group energized. Most teams begin on an emotional high. You want to maintain that high interest level.

61. Make sure your project contributes to the organization's bottom line.

62. Build positive relationships with other managers. They can support your objective in the high councils of the organization.

63. Maintain regular communication with the team's sponsor. Think of him or her as the team's internal customer and treat your sponsor accordingly.

64. Produce compelling reports and presentations that convince senior management of the need to pursue the team's recommendations.

60. Keep the Group Energized

Most members are enthusiastic when first asked to join a team effort. They see it as an opportunity to share their ideas, network within the organization, and increase their visibility and consequently their promotability. But over time it is easy for team members to lose interest, as team participation takes up time that they could be spending on their day-to-day jobs.

A high-value manager monitors member enthusiasm and acts when it starts to wane.

61. Contribute to the Bottom Line

To keep interest in the project high, you need to demonstrate to the group that the team has the attention of senior management and that the objective of the team is important to the company. Invite the sponsor and other top executives to attend team sessions where individual members' contributions can be highlighted. A story in your company's in-house newsletter can also help. You might want, too, to place in a visible area of the workplace a chart that shows team progress. Not only does this let members know that the goal of the project is getting closer, but it communicates to the rest of the organization what the team is doing for it, giving the visibility members wanted when they joined the group.

Sometimes a problem is limited to one or two members. If the individual is failing to complete his or her assignments on schedule, then a counseling session may be in order. But sometimes it is just a decline in interest that is hard to define but evident in other changes: in the level of creativity exhibited, in punctuality, or in the level of concentration at the session. Too insignificant for counseling but demanding of some attention.

The first step would be to identify the reason for the change in attitude. Meet with the person(s) to probe for reasons why enthusiasm about the project is waning. If the problem is tied to the direction the team is taking—the action plan doesn't reflect the member's thinking—you might want to surface it before the problem spreads. Handle likewise a problem related to team leadership; maybe the member feels that you are rushing too quickly to a solution or moving too slowly. If it is a lack of time to devote to both the job and team effort and the individual's knowledge is critical to the team, you may want to find ways to free the person from some of his or her regular work to spend needed time on the project. A meeting with his or her manager may be called for to come up with some possible solutions to the problem.

In some cases, the person may not know the reason for decreasing interest in the project. In that case, you may have to find out a little more about this team member—particularly what motivates him or her and whether that may be affecting team participation.

People have different needs, as Abraham Maslow's Hierarchy of Needs tells us. Psychologist Maslow developed a pyramidal hierarchy that reflects those factors that most motivate people. At the bottom of the hierarchy are physiological needs, which are our most basic needs for shelter and food and those most easily satisfied. Moving up the pyramid, there are security needs, then belonging, self-esteem, and finally self-actualizing needs. Security is related to retaining our job and issues of safety, while belonging ties to our need for social relationships. Self-esteem needs involve our sense of self-worth. At the top of the pyramid is self-actualizing, which relates to our need to realize our full potential. Steve Friedland of Friedland & Associates, a human resources development company located in Forest Knolls, California, has used the hierarchy as a tool for improved team facilitation, but the hierarchy can also be used to reenergize bored team members as the project is in the performing or mature phase.

- *Physiological needs.* Team member performance is not likely to be influenced by physiological needs. If a team's goal might lead to such drastic change that a person might be without food or shelter, then physiological needs might be triggered, but more likely the loss of job would affect:

- *Security needs.* If an individual joins a team only to discover that the end result of the effort might be a restructuring of the workplace, with the possibility of layoffs, including his or her termination, then fear about the team project's continuation might surface. Offering reassurances may be insufficient; the potential for drastic change may be so frightening that the member(s) may drag their feet. All you may be able to do is to swear those who are change-adverse to secrecy and continue the project with those remaining diehards.

Security needs are also threatened when someone becomes involved in a team effort and becomes concerned about the impact of failure of the project on his or her career. If that is the case, try to mitigate fears by reviewing progress to date, assessing concerns one-on-one and in the group, redirecting the group when needed, even renegotiating the team's overall goals with senior management if necessary. For instance, the team has been created to develop a new product line but market data suggest that extensions to the existing products would be more favorably received by the marketplace. The team members are reluctant to pursue the mission as set forth by management, but the group has a number of excellent ideas for ancillary products that it feels could substantially improve the organization's bottom line. Agreement from management to change the mission could put the entire group on a new, more positive course and reinvigorate the entire team effort.

▪ *Belonging.* Some people will volunteer to join a team because of their need to feel a part of a group. They look forward to the socialization among members. But some teams meet, then part, and between sessions do not get together. When belongers don't get the socialization they expected, they may exhibit indifference to the team process. It may not be sufficient to conduct a counseling session, but it could affect the timetable or results of the team effort. Where you suspect this could be behind a decline in an individual's interest in the team, you may want to provide opportunities for members to socialize. The rapport that could develop will not only address the needs of belongers but also create a more productive creative climate.

▪ *Self-esteem.* Some people see team membership as evidence of greater worth to the organization. When the team doesn't get the visibility they anticipated, and they in turn don't see their value increase in the eyes of the organization, they lose interest in the effort, threaten to drop out, and in the process demoralize the rest of the group. High visibility for the project and the team can keep those with strong self-esteem needs satisfied and productive, as high-value managers know.

▪ *Self-actualization.* Those members who would like to fully utilize their creativity and problem-solving skills are the self-actualizers, and they join for the opportunity to demonstrate their capabilities and gain recognition. These individuals have to feel that their contributions are appreciated and that they are making a difference. They grow dissatisfied when they work on projects that begin with lots of fanfare then seem to go nowhere or when they do considerable work but receive no recognition. A high-value manager likely has strong self-actualization needs so he or she can relate to the feelings of such high actualizers. While a team leader can't do the impossible, he or she will network to overcome political and other obstacles in the way of the team. High-value managers also know the value of recognition and will give recognition to team members who go beyond their assignments to achieve the team's goal. Praise for a well-done job goes a long way toward sustaining team involvement. Teachers nod their heads and respond, "Good," when students speak up in class. There are ways you as leader can show members that you value your members' contribution.

Showing Your Appreciation

Consider Helen, a manager, who began showing her appreciation for her team on the very first day her team came together. She explained to the group's members that they had been chosen because they were, in her opinion, the most creative individuals within the organization. In subsequent meetings, she walked that talk by moving among the group during brainstorming, walking toward members as they spoke, using open body gestures, eye contact, and a smile to demonstrate how much she appreciated their contributions.

Look at your team members. How would you define their needs? Take a piece of paper and draw a pyramid, and place each member in the right position within the pyramid. (See Figure 14–1.) Keep their primary position on the hierarchy in mind to sustain their interest through the life of the project. You might also consider it when giving assignments. For instance, someone who is motivated primarily by belonging needs probably knows the names of individuals throughout the organization to go to for information to help the team. Those with self-esteem needs or self-actualizing needs are best assigned to projects where they can demonstrate their worth and creativity to the group. High actualizers especially need the kinds of assignments that will allow them to get the recognition they crave.

Figure 14-1. Maslow's Hierarchy of Needs.

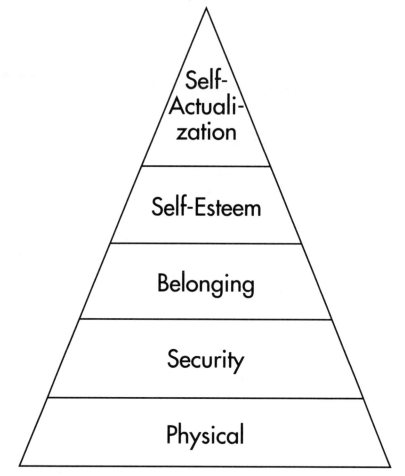

62. Build Positive Relationships With Other Managers

If your team includes staff from other departments, you want these members' supervisors to appreciate the importance of the team effort. When they do, they will be more receptive to requests like more staff time from team members from their departments. Update senior staff regularly to convince them to stay committed to your project. It will also make it easier to request help because your fellow managers will believe that what you are doing will benefit everyone in the end.

Of course, the most cooperative colleagues will be those who can see a direct benefit to their own operation from accomplishment of the team goal. So when a relationship exists between a peer's needs or concerns and the expected results of the project, you need to emphasize that. In a way, you are practicing a form of consultative selling; that is, you are selling not the end result of the team effort but the benefit or impact that end result can have on the manager's operation.

Needless to say, this kind of selling demands that your own scope not be limited to your department's boundaries. Besides being knowledgeable about your role in your company's strategic direction, you need to be aware of other managers' responsibilities in achieving that future vision. If a particular team decision will affect a colleague's operation, then you need to alert him or her to the fact, even invite him to the team meeting in which the issue will be discussed. Even if the final decision is contrary to his plans, being invited to represent his viewpoint will build feelings of trust between you and him that extend beyond the project's life.

In some instances, however, you may have to depend on your personal influence with a colleague rather than on the relationship between your team's mission and the company's strategic intent, to gain his or her support of the team objectives. The project's sponsor may not have the power base to force another manager to support your efforts. Or the project may affect only your department's operation.

If your image is one of someone who sees peers solely as competitors, then it's unlikely you will be able to get help from any colleague. But if you have the trust of your peers and are known as someone who will help others out when the need arises, then the possibility of a manager's extending a hand to you and your team is much greater. Cooperation is usually returned in kind.

Keep in mind that good collegial relations aren't built solely on offers of help—assigning a staff member to help the head of another department, working extra hours to get a customer order out in time, and the like. You can also build good relations through empathetic listening in which the information exchanged is kept in confidence, the colleague is encouraged, and ideas are exchanged.

Don't wait until the need exists to build positive work relationships with fellow managers. Begin now. Besides preparing for a time when you might need to ask for help, good relationships between peers make the workday go more smoothly. Ask yourself these questions:

- Do I believe that my fellow managers will be cooperative, and do I act toward them accordingly?
- When asked to lend people or provide expertise or information, and I have the resources to do so, do I share?
- Do I find opportunities outside of staff meetings to foster communication with peers (have lunch, for instance)?
- Am I known as someone who doesn't play dirty politics to get resources, professionally undercutting colleagues to win favor and advancement?
- Do I have a record of trustworthiness and reliability that makes me someone others will want to work with?
- Am I appreciative of the pressures other managers are under?
- Do I involve fellow managers in decisions that affect them?

Yes answers suggest you have already begun to build bridges to other department managers.

Go further. If you are currently heading up a team, make a list of departments whose cooperation you may need in the future. What is your current relationship with the manager in charge of each department on the list? Do you know at least one person in each critical area with whom you are on good terms? (If you aren't involved in a team effort at present, you might still want to do the exercise, but think in terms of your current department's needs and which individuals could help or hinder your plans. Yes, it's probably worthwhile to identify potential enemies, too.)

Now do one more thing. Identify those functions within the organization in which you don't know someone or in which you aren't on good terms with the person you know. As an objective over the next six months, plan to establish a good relationship with at least one person (preferably the person in charge).

As a second objective, make a commitment to regularly meet with those individuals with whom you are on good terms already. It doesn't take a major effort to send a memo of thanks when your contact in another department goes out of her way for you. Or to call to say thank you. And why not take the long way back to your office to wish someone who heads another department happy anniversary?

Turning bad working relationships around will take a little more effort on your part. Depending on what caused someone to become your enemy, it may take some time to convince the individual that there is more to be gained than lost by putting aside past differences. Although you may not necessarily be able to make the person a friend, with perseverance you should be able to develop enough of a rapport to work positively together on any project.

63. Maintain Regular Communication With the Team's Sponsor

On many occasions, a member of senior management will sponsor a team effort. You put together the team, and the team and you, in turn, fine-tune the mission and proceed to work on the project, keeping in mind conditions set by the sponsor. In a sense, your sponsor is the team's internal customer, and you have to treat this individual with the same care as you would an external customer.

You, as team leader, are responsible for keeping the sponsor informed throughout the process. You may want the sponsor to attend an occasional meeting to monitor the efforts of the group, especially if the team's efforts will significantly affect the company's bottom line. Build and maintain a good relationship with your sponsor since you may have to call on him or her to eliminate obstacles in the way of the team's goals, as Richard did in the following situation.

Getting Your Sponsor's Cooperation

Richard, learned how important his team's sponsor, Hal, was when the team needed not only additional funds to test-market a new product but a vehicle to test-market it in.

Hal oversaw Marketing, as well as Richard's department, and he was able to provide space in a catalog that mailed to the same target market as the team's new product. Richard called Hal one morning to tell him he had just learned that the group had missed the deadline for reserving catalog space by just a week. Hal was able to call the creative department, and by noon Richard received a confirmation from that department that space was available to announce the new product.

Richard had accepted the challenge of creating the new product and had received Hal's assurances that he would support the team as best he could. Richard called Hal up on that promise, and Hal came through. But remember that Richard had paved the way over the early stages of the team effort by providing regular oral reports, as well as written minutes reflecting the outcome of each team session.

Hal is a hands-on manager, and consequently had wanted to attend a few team sessions. Richard prepared agendas for these meetings that spotlighted team accomplishments as well as team members. Hal was able to see his product idea taking shape before his very eyes. Richard clearly understood the impact that successful production of this product would have on the company's bottom line. As a result, he drew the very best from each of the team members by empowering them and maintaining clear flow of information among them between meetings, thereby demonstrating his own leadership ability to Hal—and further reassuring Hal.

Upon accepting the role of team leader from Hal, Richard worked with him in creating a one-page document that identified the market for the new product, cost for production, and potential return. This document was the foundation for the group's mission statement and subsequent efforts. The group was able to identify some of the problems that previous products had encountered and shared this information with Hal, who immediately could apply the knowledge to other areas of his operation. At one session devoted to naming the new product, Hal watched as Richard and his group brainstormed.

Richard's previous track record had prompted Hal to select him to head up this project. His understanding of the problems facing Hal's existing products and his appreciation of the division's need for something unique to bring into the marketplace, assure him leadership of another team in the future.

64. Produce Compelling Reports and Presentations

Once your project is completed, you will likely have to get approval from either your sponsor or the entire management group to implement your team's recommendations. No doubt, your group will have to submit a written report, but the report may be preceded by a presentation to those with final say.

In order to sell your team's ideas, you might want to think of the report as a promotional piece rather than a white paper. Depending on the team's purpose, the report might take one of three formats:

1. *Informational reports* on a study conducted by a team should begin with a summary sentence or paragraph on the group's conclusions, followed by background information on how the team approached the research task, a paragraph or two on any questions that might exist related to the research or research data, and the group's recommendations on how that information can be applied.

2. *Interpretive reports* on a sales or marketing effort could begin with an overview or background of the situation, describe the present situation and the group's conclusions about why this situation now exists, offer recommendations of what should be done to rectify the situation or solve the problem, and conclude with the expected results.

3. *Recommendation reports*, the most frequently issued by teams, should begin with the actual recommendations. This would be followed by background information, a review of the problem and issues involved, criteria for the solution reached by the team, analysis of the various options, review of the risks that might exist, and in-depth description of the solution.

Whatever format you use, remember that any team report should answer these questions:

- What was the team's mission?
- What processes and techniques for studying the problem or reaching its conclusions were used?
- What approaches to the mission worked? Which didn't work?
- What would the team recommend the organization do differently?
- How much time will implementation of the recommendations take?
- What are the implications of taking the action? Risks? Benefits?

Note that the same report guidelines apply to any project—whether the work is done by a team or you on your own—submitting a new-product idea or improvement proposal.

While written reports should tell the total story, a presentation allows you to spotlight those points most critical for senior management. In team presentations, members can also transfer their own enthusiasm for the team's conclusions during the presentation to the movers and shakers in the organization.

Most of the time you won't have more than twenty to thirty minutes for your presentation. But there is still much that can go wrong in a few minutes so you need to plan your presentation carefully.

Remember, the purpose of your presentation is to get buy-in to your proposal or solution. As any salesperson will tell you, that entails understanding your audience and its concerns. If your group has been sponsored by a member of senior management but still needs the approval of the entire management team to proceed, you may want to consult with your sponsor, after gaining his or her input and approval to your team's recommendations.

Just as you developed the agenda for each of your team meetings, you need to create an agenda for your presentation. In creating that agenda, begin by deciding as a team on how you can all best present your team's recommendations. You want to tie all your comments to the same operating problem or strategic thrust—e.g., dollar savings, customer satisfaction, market expansion, product extension, or what have you. If you don't agree in advance, each member might focus on some smaller aspect of the mission, thus drawing attention away from the total group's mission and action plan.

Visual aids can add to your presentation, sustaining your audience's interest. But keep them simple. They should support member remarks, not distract from them.

To make sure that each presenter stays within his or her allocated time, you should do several run-throughs of the entire presentation. All team members should be asked to provide an outline of their remarks and share it with the team as a whole before fleshing the outline out.

Needless to say, no one should read from a prepared paper. Well-prepared outlines with key words to trigger thoughts should be sufficient after practice, practice, practice.

Like the best sales appeals, the best presentations are those that follow the "tell-em" approach; that is, they tell the audience what it is going to be told, then make the points they promised to make, then conclude by telling the audience what it was told (the format for a recommendation report, too). The presentations should make a point, provide background to support that point, then move on to the second point, support that point, then move on to point three, and so on.

You should have your team members keep the points they will make in their individual presentations down to a reasonable number in relation to the time they have to make their case.

As team leader, you will be opening the presentation, identifying the team's mission and its conclusions. At the end of the program, you will close by recapping, driving home the team's recommendations with a "call to action." That call should be built on the work undertaken by your team and, once again, reflect your customer's—that is, your sponsor's or top management's—needs.

Be prepared for a Q&A session after the presentation, even practicing fielding questions thrown at the group by the sponsor. Like any salesperson, you want to get closure, and a good Q&A session can provide that. Assuming that your promotional literature—your team's written report—matches the quality of the presentation, you will end the team effort on a positive note.

Before making the presentation, check the meeting room to be sure that ventilation and lighting are adequate and that the seating arrangement reflects your purpose. For instance, if you want to encourage an exchange of opinion and greater sense of camaraderie between your team members and the audience, you might want to use a round or rectangular table at which your group would sit with its audience. If you plan a more formal presentation, you might want to arrange your team at the front of the room, with the audience chairs set up as in a classroom.

Arrange in advance for flip charts, projection equipment, sound equipment, pencils and blank paper, and the like, and check prior to the meeting to see that everything has been arranged as you instructed. Prepare a written agenda and distribute it at the start of the meeting. If senior management needs to prepare for the meeting, send any background information in advance of the session.

Start your meetings on time. Follow the same rules that you followed in running team sessions. Adhere to the agenda and time allocated for each agenda item, rather than let the meeting run out of control.

Whatever the reaction of senior management, this wrap-up meeting is an excellent opportunity to do some selling about the members of the team—and yourself. Use this opportunity to give recognition to the group. Monetary awards might be the best acknowledgment of a job well done, but a high-value manager knows that publicity in the company newsletter, a note in personnel files, a group luncheon or dinner, or some special gift like a team pin or paperweight, if funds are short, is a nice way of saying thank you to all the members and maintaining the positive relationship built over the team sessions.

Section V
Life Skills

We all know managers who work hard and do their jobs well yet do not advance in their careers. No matter how successful they are in their jobs, their careers fail to reflect their abilities. What holds many back is their inability to work smart through better time management, balance the stresses that make up their workdays, and take charge of their career through targeted networking and career planning. We call these "life skills," and in this final section of the book we examine the core career competencies needed to thrive, let alone stay employed, in today's world of diminished job security.

As a high-value manager, you need skills beyond those that allow you to increase productivity, build customer or quality awareness, anticipate problems in the making, and solve existing problems on your own or through team efforts. You need to know how to achieve your career goals. Interviews with successful mid-career professionals have enabled us to identify those life skills that will enable you to juggle the multiple priorities and other stresses that are a part of today's leaner organizations, to advance your career by networking both within and outside your organization, and to develop and implement career plans as successfully as you develop and implement your operating plans. Mastering these skills will allow you to leverage your job skills for professional advancement.

15

"It's Already Afternoon!"

Do you sometimes feel that everybody controls your time but you? Senior management? Your employees? Your customers? Even your vendors? This lack of control over your own time means not only that critical tasks aren't getting done but that you always feel stressed. Which, in turn, influences your productivity and the quality of the decisions you make. No one can think clearly when in a constant state of anxiety due to pressing work.

The situation in which you find yourself is understandable. Time has always been a resource in short supply for managers, but never has it been so scarce as in today's lean organizations, in which fewer managers are doing as much or more than was done in the past. So, before offering advice on time and stress management, we want to acknowledge that your workload may be unreasonably heavy and that we know of no miracle cure. Still, there are techniques available to the high-value manager to give you greater control over the use of your time and help you relieve some of the stress that comes with the job of manager.

To be one of those managers who will succeed in the leaner workplace, you must know these techniques and consequently:

65. Work smart by thinking through any task before beginning. Responding to a situation without planning can cause you to approach it ineffectively or inefficiently, thereby wasting time and money.

66. Prioritize work to focus on critical tasks.

67. Use subgoals and deadlines to better organize your use of your time.

68. Know how to say no—without alienating those seeking your aid—to requests for help that will distract from your most important responsibilities. On the other hand, know when to say yes and when to say maybe.

69. Know how to avoid the traditional time wasters. Develop good time management habits.

70. Pace yourself so that the stress of today's heavier workloads has a minimal effect on the quality of your life and job performance. Understand your own personal energy peaks and valleys and use that information to most efficiently and effectively complete projects.

65. Work Smart—Think Before You Act

A lot of managers carry such heavy workloads that they habitually plunge into one assignment after another without little thought as to how the tasks should best be handled or what work they should do immediately and what work can wait. They are working harder and faster than ever before but not necessarily more productively, because they spend too little time in thinking through each task first. A multitude of tasks pile up, and they all seem to be labeled "urgent." The end result is that too much time is spent putting out fires instead of preventing them. Strategic time management and effective communication can go a long way toward preventing forest fires.

The Cost of Not Planning

Connie, the head of Office Services, is a champion firefighter. She comes to work with certain objectives in mind but her plans never seem to withstand the office reality—that is, the constant telephone calls, the visitors who are there either for information or a chat, the unexpected task from the boss, or demand for an expense account report already several days overdue. Still, Connie does a lot of good work, right?

A broken office copier wasn't fixed because Connie forgot to call the service firm. Consequently, no copies could be made of a proposal to be sent to a key customer, the proposal went out a day late, and the company almost lost the account. Management asked Connie to work with the Systems group to identify wiring needs for a new computer mainframe. Rushing down the hall, Connie thought the head of Systems had said they would meet at two on Wednesday. No, he had said the meeting would be at three on Tuesday. Systems called on Tuesday to find out where she was, but she had just rushed off to put out another fire. Connie completed the blueprints for reorganizing a portion of the workplace ahead of deadline. She proudly presented them to her boss, who was glad she had done it but more concerned about the projected budget for the renovation he had asked her to complete about a month before. Unfortunately, the budget was needed to decide who was to move where, so it was very likely that the blueprints would have to be re-executed.

Admittedly, the situation isn't all Connie's fault. She suffers from a department that is short-staffed and a work environment in which an occasional special project comes down from senior management that demands great chunks of her time. But she could avoid some of the problems if she planned her work better, was more skilled at time management, and used clear objectives in handling her work. So could all of us.

While nothing can be done about the staff situation or workload, when work is out of control you may be able to get out from under by proceeding methodically. Giving a little thought to a situation may enable you to identify a smarter way to handle a problem or situation. More work or longer hours aren't the only—or best—solutions to every problem you will encounter on the job. When faced with a last-minute job, pause for a moment. Count to ten before acting. Taking a breath or two before acting may be sufficient to prevent needless wheel spinning and unnecessary pressure. You will have time to consider how the task can be done more efficiently or more effectively. Maybe work can be outsourced? Perhaps there is another, less expensive way to accomplish your objective? If time is the scarce resource, then there may be a firm that can make up lost time in delivery to your customer?

Stopping to catch your breath will also enable you to determine if what you have in front of you is a real crisis. Determine what warrants a frantic pace and what can be done in due time, and respond accordingly. Certainly, don't allow someone who is insecure about your ability to complete a task on time to throw your own priorities out of whack. A realistic view of what is a crisis allows you to make decisions about how to spend your time. Learn to prioritize.

66. Prioritize Your Tasks

A high-value manager looks at the workload and determines those tasks that really need to be completed *now*. These are your priorities. If you have some confusion about what your priorities are, you're not alone. Priorities can change daily in today's ever changing workplace. So periodically talk to your boss about where you should be putting your major effort. Make sure your employees are aware of the department's priorities as well. One way to do this is to tie priorities and employee performance together in the standards or goals set as a part of the performance appraisal process, allocating x proportion of the final rating to each priority based on its importance. The standards you and your boss set for you can be the blueprint for developing your staff members' goals.

Before you begin your conversation with your boss, here are some questions you might want to ask yourself. Bring the list with you, too, during the goal-setting meeting with your boss to compare your answers to his or hers:

- How is my operation expected to contribute to the company's strategic plan?
- What is seen as the department's key roles or responsibilities?
- In what ways can we support other areas of the business that are critical to the strategic plan?
- How can we better service internal clients? External clients? Contribute to the organization's image as a high-quality, high-service business?
- Are there any problems—with people or work—that require immediate attention?
- What is the department not currently doing that senior management would like it to do now or in the near future?

We have talked about operating with a sense of purpose—the difference between busywork and results-oriented tasks. Too much attention to busywork is a case of too much sawdust and not enough boards. Answers to these questions will assure your focus and that of your entire operation are on issues critical to the company's competitive advantage.

Once you know those activities and issues that are important to the company, you can plan each workday better. Maybe you most enjoy talking and meeting with your customers, but if your customer reps are having problems with the current telephone service or one or two reps are not as familiar as they should be with company product, then your time is better spent making a case for a new telephone system or training your reps. Or you might prefer to fine-tune an idea you have for a new product, but differences between your product managers may demand you put your attention first on the interpersonal relationships between staff members if the disputes are affecting productivity.

When you've done these more important tasks, you can work on that new-product idea or make some calls to customers. These are important tasks, too, and deserve your time. But don't waste your time on insignificant chores. Treat time as an asset for which you want a return on investment for every minute spent.

Know that your management ability won't be measured by the quantity of time you spend on the job. Time spent on chores that could have been delegated to staff is wasted, with no return. But hours spent on projects tied to profit improvement issues or safety or service or quality are well invested.

Don't just think through how you will spend the day. Write your priorities down for each day. This way you are less likely to get distracted. At the end of the day, or in the morning before work (but always during nonworking hours, when you can relax and concentrate), write down everything you have to do during the coming day, and when you're going to do it. Don't be too ambitious. Try to be as realistic as you can. Leave some room for emergencies and unexpected interruptions.

A priorities list is very different from a to-do list. A to-do list is just that—a list of all the tasks you must, ought to, and could do. A priorities list orders your tasks in terms of importance.

The size of a task isn't indicative of its importance. Some small tasks can be essential. But no matter how critical, these smaller chores can be easily forgotten—sometimes not only due to their size but also to how we become responsible for doing them. We walk through the office, or we visit with a colleague, or we meet with a customer. In the course of our travels, we may be asked to provide some information essential to someone else doing a report, to call our distributor to check on an upcoming shipment, or to sign off on a mechanical we had been asked to review. These are tasks that can easily slip our mind. To be sure that they don't get neglected, carry a small notebook or 3-by-5 inch cards with you on which you note phone calls to be made or returned, information to be obtained, reminders about a letter to be sent, and the like.

If possible, try to complete one priority before you start another. Say you have three things that need to get done today, three things to be done by week's end, and three to be done in a month or so. Take the three "today" items and determine which is the most important. Start in on Project 1 and stick with it until it's done, touching nothing else. Then go to Project 2 and follow the same procedure. But sometimes you'll get stuck at a certain point by circumstances beyond your control: For instance, you can go no further on Project 1 until Sam returns your call. In that case—but only in that case—start on Project 2. But drop it and go back to Project 1 as soon as Sam gives you the information you need to continue on the first project.

67. Use Subgoals and Deadlines

Don't be intimidated by large projects. In general, things will go faster if you divide a large task into several small ones. Set deadlines for each subgoal as well as the finished project to monitor your progress.

There are computer software programs that will help you to track progress on larger assignments, even alert you to deadlines, not to mention notify you about a meeting you are scheduled to attend in ten minutes. But if you don't have the computer software, you might try a trick like this we read about. Analyze the project and divide it into smaller tasks. Now mark on a three-months-at-a-glance calendar a due date for completion of each of these smaller tasks. If you have several long-term projects, use different-colored markers. Use colored dots to alert you to the days on which the final projects are due. Place the calendar where it is visible to you at your desk.

This way you will see at a glance how you stand with some of your major assignments.

Admittedly, if you are juggling several projects at once, and see subgoal deadlines pass with nothing done, this technique can bring on feelings of anxiety. But that should be a signal that something is wrong with your use of time. Then, as a high-value manager, you have to ask how realistic the deadlines were. Maybe you set impossible-to-meet deadlines. Or you may have had the time but squandered it on less important tasks. You may want to maintain a log of how you use your time to see how well you manage this important asset.

Most of us know all the rules of good time management, but we have a hard time following them. Some people need to get the clutter of smaller chores out of the way before they can truly focus on more-important issues. If you fall into this category, you might want to consider delegating more of the less important tasks to free your mind to focus on critical subgoals and major projects.

When you aren't being pulled in many directions, it is easier to block time during the day to work on a subgoal or a project. If you block time over several days or weeks on your calendar to work on the project, and stick to your schedule, you will find the major project completed on the day it is due.

68. Know How to Say No

Having your priorities straight makes it easier to deal with requests for help from a fellow manager or even your boss. That is because you will know that you have to say no to any requests that will keep you from achieving the goals you are supposed to achieve.

In handling requests for help, don't concentrate solely on your priorities. There will be occasions when you will want to help your fellow managers. Still, there will be others when you just can't spare the time.

The secret of turning down a request without alienating the person asking for help—even a request from your boss—is knowing how to say no. The best response is, "I'd like to help if I can fit it into my schedule." Then go on to explain that you have other tasks that have to take priority. You aren't rejecting the person or his or her request—it's the truth. The bottom line: Courtesy and kindness, combined with truth, win out.

If it's just a matter of time—and you don't have it now but you might have it later—and you would like to help your colleague, offer to help if the person can wait a few days. But if that isn't acceptable, then be firm in refusing. Don't equivocate. If you say you might be able to help just to get the person off your back, then fail to come through as promised, you can ruin your reputation with this person—and maybe the whole management team when the tale is told, and it will be. And that can have repercussions later on. As mentioned in Chapter 13, when you need help from a colleague and offer a horse trade, you have to have a reputation for credibility to make a deal.

If the request comes from your boss, then the burden is on him or her to decide whether this new request takes precedence over those priorities you have agreed on earlier. If your boss is willing to give you more time to complete your current work to free you to handle this new priority, then say yes to the assignment. But most frequently, your boss will reconsider the request, freeing you to finish what you were already doing.

You might also agree to take on extra work, even with a full plate, when the new task is tied to previously identified top priorities; when you are knowledgeable enough about the subject to complete the task in a very short time (that is, you have all the facts and information at your fingertips, if not already stored in your brain); when you can depend on others (like the person making the request or your own staff) to give you a hand; or when your boss will accept the cost of contracting for extra help or paying for staff overtime to allow you and your staff to satisfy the request.

Perhaps the most important factor in allowing you to take on, and manage well, extra work is how you have trained your staff and your own attitude toward last-minute assignments. How flexible are you and your staff? If you and they have learned to see rush jobs or sudden requests as challenges, not ever continuing problems, you are more likely to take on and do these chores well. You may experience some stress but it will be of the positive kind—from a challenging job done well.

69. Avoid Traditional Time Wasters

Actually, it's not work that takes up the most time in our workdays; it's the time wasters that have nothing to do with our jobs. To avoid using time poorly:

■ *Don't overpractice an open-door policy.* You want to be accessible to staff and senior management—even an unexpected customer or fellow manager—but that shouldn't prevent you from getting your own work done. So set up a schedule that makes you inaccessible for so many hours per day or week—enough time for you to focus on key projects. Don't get caught up in the concept of an open-door to the point where you are too accessible to visitors who want to stop by to chat. Your staff and colleagues should know you are available, but they also need to know that your time is precious and you need some time alone, behind a closed door, to get that work done. After all, there would be no reason to have a door if you didn't need to close it once in a while to do productive work—not just personnel counseling.

■ *Do limit visitors' time.* When you have a visitor, try to set a time limit on the visit. "I'd like to help. But I have only fifteen minutes. Can we get it done in that time?" Set the limit and stick to it. If more time is needed, then make an appointment to address the problem at a later time.

If someone wants to see you and you know that it is always difficult to get that person out of your office, another way to keep the visiting time down is to meet at his or her workplace or office. Then you can more easily end the conversation by pointing to other tasks awaiting you at your desk and leave.

Standing when an unexpected visitor drops by is another way to keep control over visiting time. If you want to continue the discussion, all you have to do is sit down. If you have work that must be done, you can answer the visitor's question or schedule a time when you can do so, maybe even at his or her office.

- *Don't allow a "short" visit to grow longer and longer. . . .* You are both seated, and what seemed unlikely to take long is taking an excessive amount of time, demanding both greater attention and time. Suggest meeting later. Admit that you have your mind on other goals right now, and reschedule so you can give the issue the time and attention it truly deserves.

- *Don't become a victim of paperwork.* Sometimes the most mundane of chores, like routine reports, employee evaluations, expense reports, and so forth, seem to take up the most time. The only way to keep paperwork under control is to plan for it. Set aside time each day to deal with reports or other ongoing paperwork; doing it daily keeps it from piling up. There will still be an occasional crisis associated with some piece of paper that senior management needs immediately, but such events are easier handled when other documentation has been done on schedule.

Paperwork has a knack of growing out of control. The new office technology may have eliminated a lot of the paper but it certainly hasn't done away with the paperwork. Think just about e-mail and the number of messages you get daily. Because of the nature of the messages—written in telegraphic style—they seem to demand we read and respond immediately to each one as it arrives. But a better approach is to set aside the first fifteen minutes in the morning and the first fifteen minutes after lunch to answer e-mail. Likewise, traditional correspondence.

If you are fortunate enough to have an assistant, ask him or her to open and sort your mail. Don't stack unread magazines or newsletters on your desk. The clutter will only add to your feelings of urgency. Rather, have your assistant go through the table of contents and clip critical items and maintain files on these subjects for your later review. Ask that incoming correspondence and reports also be sorted in terms of priorities or by projects to make review of your mail faster.

70. Pace Yourself to Manage Stress

No matter how well you manage your time, today's workplace is a stressful environment. So you had better learn to deal with stress.

We're talking about negative stress here. As we mentioned, there is also positive stress—like an exciting project that allows you to demonstrate your talents. But the stress that has the most impact on your health, not to mention the quality of your job performance, is the negative variety, due to such forces as an unattainable promotion; too heavy a workload; uncertainty about what is expected of you; conflict with your bosses, coworkers, employees, even family; and competing organizational goals and interpersonal communication problems.

You know you are experiencing work-related stress when each of these statements is reflective of your situation:

1. I feel like I am interrupted too often.
2. I feel like I'm on a treadmill moving from one deadline to another.
3. At home, I feel pressured about work. At work, I feel pressured about home issues.
4. I take work home every day.
5. My workday is made up of interruptions interrupted by further interruptions.
6. I don't know what is expected of me.
7. I worry about just how good a job I'm doing.
8. I feel I can't spend the time with my staff that they need.
9. I am so busy fighting fires that I know I'm unaware of the things I need to know to get the day-to-day work done.
10. My desk is stacked with paper, and I have no idea where to begin.

To help minimize the stress that stems from overwork, the best advice is to learn to pace yourself. The most successful managers are those who have learned to go on superdrive for a period, then slow down for a time, then speed up once more, and at the end of the day take a break. Relax with a hobby, book, or favorite sitcom. Or unwind by taking a walk or even playing softball with the neighborhood team.

In the office, when faced with a particularly stressful situation, calm the body and the soul and avoid exhausting yourself by taking a walk around the block. If you don't want to leave the office, do your own copying at the office copier. Besides giving you a moment to relax, you may pick up some information that is valuable to your work. (The office copiers and network printers have replaced the old water coolers as the place to mingle and pick up interoffice information.)

Try to avoid high-pressure lunches. Instead, seek out on-the-job friends to share your meals with. It's less stressful on your digestive system, and may even give you a chance to get another viewpoint on a situation or to vent, both of which are critical in these high-stress times.

Consider, too, your personal body rhythms. Facing a major project when your natural body rhythm is down adds to the stress of completing the project. So ask yourself: When do you feel most productive? Least productive? When is it easiest for you to do a task? When is it toughest? Try to keep a record over a period of days, then try to adjust your work schedule so you do the most stressful tasks when your energy is at its highest peaks. When it is lowest, tackle the less stressful tasks.

While most people are at their best first thing in the morning, don't assume that you are. If you only begin to get fired up around midmorning, set aside that time of the day to devote to your top projects. Completion of your high-priority tasks will give you a sense of accomplishment on which you can build the rest of the workday. What if you find you are most productive about the time everyone is getting ready to head home, then save your key tasks for then, perhaps staying a little later in the office when everything is quiet to complete the work. It will give you a lift knowing you've done the work when you arrive the next morning. Increasing use of flextime allows you to make most productive use of your knowledge of your personal body rhythms.

The important thing is not to use your most productive times on simpler jobs, putting off that major job to "first thing in the morning" or whenever.

You can reduce the stresses you feel, too, by changing stressful situations when you can. What incidents or situations occur regularly that contribute to your feelings of stress? If you can do so, try to control or eliminate them. For instance, if you have a critical task but a mediocre performer to do it, you might want to assign a better worker to that key task until you have had time to coach or counsel (or, yes, maybe terminate) that employee.

Try to put people and situations into perspective. When you look at each situation as a matter of life and death, you can develop tremendous feelings of stress. Ask yourself, "What is the worst that could happen if I don't complete this project on schedule? Would the world end?" No. "Would I lose my job?" Unlikely. "Would my boss think less of me?" Perhaps, but more time taken might also produce a better-quality report or analysis, which might be well received. Sometimes all you need to do is alert your boss sufficiently in advance that "I may be delayed in completing a project because. . . ." Frame your own questions to evaluate potentially stressful situations and help keep overreaction to a minimum.

Don't try to be perfect or outdo everyone. Trying to be perfect in everything is not only self-defeating but it's stressful. It may be controversial to say so at a time when companies are pushing the concept of total quality, but the reality is that we can't always do "outstanding" work; sometimes we have to "settle" occasionally for good work if it allows us to do several other, equally important jobs well. Even major corporations recognize that there is a point at which effort at increasing service or product quality has diminishing value.

Besides being realistic about all you can do, be realistic about your career expectations. Stress often is the result of a mismatch between an individual's career expectations and their job environment. Venting your frustration and exercising may relieve some of the tension that comes from the situation, but the only real remedies are to seek advancement elsewhere or to learn to live with your situation. Talk it out with friends and family. Don't let your frustrations bottle up inside you.

Just as you might develop a career plan or action plan to address a job problem, develop an action plan to help you handle your feelings of stress. Relaxation can help to temper stress. Time away from the stressful situation—a quiet room where you can get comfortable, shut your eyes, and free your mind of all stressful thoughts—should help reduce the tension if done about ten to twenty minutes once or twice a day. A walk around the block is another relaxing activity, as we said. Extended over a period of twenty minutes at a rigorous pace, walking is also a fine exercise, and exercise has been found to be one of the most effective means of dealing with stress if regularly practiced. Choose that exercise you like the most, check with your doctor, then go to it.

Plan this kind of program with the same detail and organization that you bring to every task. Use your free time to relax and reenergize as productively as you use your work time to do those tasks most important to your organization, your department, and you.

16

Networking and Political Know-How

As companies move toward more integrated approaches to work and managerial responsibilities become boundaryless, the worth of strong networking skills and organizational savvy has grown.

High-value managers understand how to use interpersonal relationships to win support for themselves or their teams. Network participants can help move a request along or build support for a new procedure, program, or product. Let's say that you need a sales report done monthly, rather than quarterly, but to do that you need the support of Systems. You've asked but to no avail. The technology is there, but your needs are low priority given the other commitments of the head of Systems. But let's say one of the people you met last year at a staff meeting—and who is now a part of your network—is also a friend of the head of Systems. In the course of a phone call with your network friend, you might mention your problem about getting Systems to cooperate, stressing some of the advantages to the company in having monthly data, maybe even advantages to your friend's operation. Then you need to sit back and wait. If you were able to make a good case to your network pal, it's likely she in turn will tell her old buddy. When you go back to Systems a few weeks later, you may find that the head of Systems is more willing to discuss your request. You may not get exactly what you want, but the head of Systems may have some other options that will enable you to achieve your objective.

This is only one way that positive collegial relations will help you. You may be a team leader or be asked to complete a project that demands access to information a fellow manager has, or be required to hold a meeting that involves people from outside your department or division. Important to any of these responsibilities will be your ability to get, easily and readily, the participation of all the people you need in the organization. Don't assume that since your request is good for the organization, everyone will be eager to help. Not so. Strong collegial relationships that are at the core of your network, and organizational savvy that alerts you to where to go for help, will enable you to mobilize those key decision makers, get critical information, or reach advisers who can give you important direction in your task.

Outside the organization, the same networking and influencing behaviors will provide opportunities for promoting the company and getting key information to improve your organization's competitive position—not to mention promoting your own abilities and desire for advancement.

In the past, networks inside and outside the organization were just something that happened. But given the importance today—to both your job and your career—of having contacts, building and sustaining a network, and the subsequent power base it gives you, networking demands rigorous attention.

Although job descriptions don't include networking or political skills, you need to be able to:

71. Use positive politics to achieve objectives.

72. Cultivate a power base by building your reputation as trustworthy, results oriented, and fair-minded.

73. Build an internal network.

74. Sustain your network.

75. Build bridges to an outside network.

71. Use Positive Politics

Yes, we are advocating that you use your network to help you achieve your objective, to use your influence with one person to get that person to influence another. Rather than advocating office politics, this is taking advantage of those other sources of power that managers have that have nothing to do with your job title or job performance.

There will always be politics in large organizations. Certain individuals hold powerful, influential positions, and most of the others recognize the value of being in the good favor of those individuals. However, there is stronger value in building relationships among one another that allow you to work cooperatively with your peers in other positions and departments. These relationships must be based on mutual respect and an ability to work together toward a common vision without looking over the other one's shoulder to protect yourself against hidden motives.

The political games of the past aren't as likely to work in today's integrated, boundaryless organizations, in any event. What today's companies are looking for are team players who use their relationships with colleagues and those outside the organization for the benefit of the organization. Today's corporations are no more likely to reward those who curry favor or try to get on the good side of Mr. Success than those who limit their interactions with others on staff to the people identified in their job description but otherwise hide themselves away in their office. Those managers who will be the recipients of the rewards will be those who bring about change, and change is not something one person can accomplish on his or her own.

How Team Players Innovate

Marilyn is a nutritionist at a major Chicago hospital. She had an idea that would speed delivery of meals to the patients. Marilyn decided to bring her idea to the nursing director. A little flattery, plus a reminder about some favors due in return for some given in the past, and Fran, the nursing director, sent a memo to the nursing staff about the change in procedures. The procedures didn't account for some operational issues on some hospital floors, but the program's benefits, combined with flattery, blinded Fran to the faults. Nothing changed. Patients continued to get lukewarm coffee, warm salads, cold entrées, and melted desserts.

Fran investigated and discovered that some nursing staff simply ignored the dictate, others found they couldn't implement the procedures because of policies that already existed covering the timing of doctor or medication rounds. Admittedly, the success of Marilyn's program would have built her reputation at the hospital, but it also would have made hospital stays more tolerable for the patients. So Fran didn't give up.

After talking to some of the nursing staff, Fran suggested that she and Marilyn call a meeting of the floor nurses to discuss how food delivery and overall service to patients could be improved and to get the floor nurses' suggestions. The new plan made allowances for medical rounds. Those floor nurses who hadn't wanted to cooperate with "the dietitian's plan" were happy to support a program developed by both nursing staff and the food service department to improve patient stays. Marilyn and Fran received considerable credit, but their experience had taught them to "share the credit with the floor nurses whose ideas and cooperation made the program work," as Marilyn told the hospital administrator when he complimented her on her ingenuity.

Marilyn learned firsthand that the old political gamesmanship based on friendships, favors owed, and flattery of people in authority no longer works.

72. Cultivate a Powerbase

A certain power comes from a willingness to share credit, a desire to lend a hand as well as get a hand, and giving access to information as well as getting access to information. This kind of power stems from feelings of trust that you can earn when you:

- *Show you share the glory* with those who helped you achieve your goal.
- *Demonstrate that you can be trusted* not only to lend the hand you promised but also to keep confidential those things told by a peer or manager.
- *Give access to your outside network to help colleagues* without expecting them to give you credit. It may not be what you know but what someone you know knows that can help a fellow manager. The assistance will be readily accepted—and likely reciprocated—if it is clear that there are no strings attached.
- *Establish a successful track record.* No matter who is in your network, you need to have a reputation for getting results.
- *Don't take sides.* No matter which side you take, and no matter who wins, you eventually lose. At some point, the loser may be in a position to influence a decision affecting you and may have a long memory.
- *Allow a colleague on the other side of a negotiating table to walk away with something.* To do otherwise is to win the battle but ultimately lose the war.
- *Build a reputation of truthfulness.* Never lie to win a point or get the resources you need. If you think individual managers' memories

are long, the corporate memory is even longer. There will always be someone who will remember how you misled to win your point.

You won't be perceived as someone a fellow manager wants to add to his or her network if your own reputation has been sullied by broken promises, turf battles with colleagues, or inability to keep information confidential. And don't think a record of misdemeanors against fellow managers will be unknown to a manager who is located at another corporate facility or is a part of the operation. Tidbits like that are fodder for the managerial rumor mill; don't think there isn't one.

73. Build an Internal Network

You are attending a meeting of managers brought from various facilities and operating areas. You may know a few of the attendees but most of the managers are strangers. You have two options. You can revert to your childhood behavior of hanging out with your friends, those managers you know and already have good collegial relations with, or you can mingle with those managers you don't know. They don't have to be individuals who represent areas of the business that impact yours, although certainly you should make it a point to introduce yourself to those people from parts of the business that do affect your own department. But the point of the exercise is to get to know and be known by as many people within the organization as possible. The more people you know and over time add to your network, the more available to you and your employees will be information and help when it is needed. Don't forget, too, that circumstances change. Someone who may have nothing to do with your department today may have a significant impact on it—or on you and your position—tomorrow.

How's your Rolodex? Have you gone through it lately? Take the time soon to go through the names and numbers you've collected and take stock of how many of these people are still known to you. You will undoubtedly be able to divide the numbers into these categories: (1) people you talk to frequently, (2) people you talk to occasionally, (3) people you never talk to but you may want to in the future, and (4) people you have completely forgotten about.

Now make another category: people in your organization whom you do not know but would like to know.

Pull out your corporate telephone directory. Put a red check next to the name of each manager or employee you should know. Keep these names with checks beside them in mind when you are at the next managerial meeting or business retreat or company social event. Find an opportunity to introduce yourself to the individual. Engage in some small talk to create a bridge between you that you can use to contact the person later in the event you need his or her help. You don't want to come across as pushy—just friendly. If there is a way you can help the individual with a current problem, and he or she brings the situation up, offer to share your experience or resources. Suggest that the person call you after the meeting to obtain the specific information he or she needs.

To meet these people, it may be as simple as taking a walk around your own building and introducing yourself to the person you would like to meet. Most people will not turn their back on someone from their own organization who says something like, "I've heard you were an expert on _____ or, I heard you did a great job on _____. I'm John, I work in Production."

The managers who are best at networking listen more than they talk. They give others the chance to express their needs. Which helps them to build that bridge to future communications. But what they hear may also help them with a problem they have been unable to resolve. A two-way exchange of information also enables both parties to close white space, to explore issues they may both be considering, find ways they can work together to help each other, discover problems with ideas they are currently considering.

74. Sustain Your Network

As you build your network of colleagues, recognize that networking is a give-and-take relationship. If someone within your network needs your help, render it. If you need help, ask for it.

Today's office technology makes it much easier than in the past to keep a network relationship alive and well. Actually, you don't need to move out from behind your desk. You can e-mail the engineering manager in the downtown facility or fax that colleague from Brussels you met last year at a corporate annual meeting. True, there is a time commitment, but the benefit—expanding your influencing ability—is well worth it.

How do you measure the quality of an existing network relationship? Is it enough to talk to someone frequently? No. That doesn't guarantee that he or she is as valuable a contact as you might presume. It's not enough just to know someone and be on friendly terms. A truly valuable contact meets all or some of the following criteria:

- The individual will call on you when he or she is in need of your help or hears that you need some assistance.
- The individual is trustworthy enough to give you advice on a project based on his or her own experience, or to listen quietly to you as you vent about a problem you have.
- The individual is knowledgeable and skilled in an area that is useful to you.

It is possible to talk to someone on a daily basis without going beyond the business you need to discuss. Cultivating individuals in order to build a network requires that you take the next step to build a more personal rapport. You don't need to become fast friends, but rather take the time in your daily talk to extend your conversation by both sympathizing with the difficulties of your contact's operation and revealing some of your own vulnerabilities and expressing some of the problems you encounter that he or she may well be able to connect with.

Even if the two of you aren't from the same functional discipline or business, you may be able to discover a different type of bond that will cement your relationship and make it valuable to both. It could be a similar life experience, or it may more possibly be that you have compatible styles of dealing with stressful or high-pressure situations at work. It is only by letting down your guard ever so slightly that you will be able to reveal your own style and therefore open the possibility of developing a business relationship that will work for you in the future.

Are there some people you know in the organization and talk to occasionally but really don't know? Why aren't they a part of your network? Occasional contacts can often slip by you without being recognized for their importance. Yes, you know Bill in Shipping, but will Bill go out of his way for you when you need a favor? Certainly all coworkers appreciate being treated respectfully and fairly. But when your dealings with someone at work are minimal, try to make a favorable impression each time you do speak. And remember, too, that networking is a two-way street. It's not enough to recognize that someone is useful to you and to treat him or her courteously in hopes that you will be appreciated. Look also into how you can make it a truly reciprocal relationship and even go as far as offering a service or favor to that individual in order to prove that your relationship is equally beneficial to him or her.

In any network relationship, in which you have lent a hand, don't expect an immediate payback, whether it is in the form of a real hand or information or the name of another person on your network who can help. Often the return isn't in the same form as the help, anyway. Certainly don't leave the person you helped with a feeling that he or she is beholden to you. That kind of attitude will only tear down the bridge you are trying to build with this person, not strengthen it. Rather, you should behave as if your assistance was a gesture of help to a colleague, nothing more. But recognize that in the process you are selling your worth to members of your network, and the long-term payback could be unlimited.

As we said, networking is a reciprocal relationship, so you shouldn't be embarrassed about accepting help from another. Actually, not using your network for that purpose can put that bridge between you and your colleague on as shaky a foundation as your not lending him or her help when the need arises.

And don't forget to preach to staff members about the value of networking—which you prove in both your deeds and words.

A Great but Flawed Network

Billi is on good terms with most of the managers in her organization. This makes her job as director of customer service of Soft Ware, a software computer firm, much easier. When problems arise about a shipment to a customer, all Billi has to do is call Mac to get his help. Mac heads up Shipping. Terry, director of marketing, keeps Billi informed about all new products so Billi's staff is able to answer customer questions about new products as soon as they are unveiled by the sales force. Incidentally, Pete, who heads up that sales force, is also a part of Billi's network. She tracks customer reaction to the firm's software products, and he lets her know what's happening in the field. Terry is also in this loop and welcomes feedback from Billi on customer reaction to each new product as well as existing ones.

Companies have certain strengths that make them stand out. Distributors who carried the firm's products thought that Soft Ware's strength lay in its targeted customer line. But the source of the company's success wsa actually the information network that these key managers had created.

But recently Billi had to have heart surgery. Her long hospital visit would be followed by three months of recuperation.

Mike, Billi's assistant, agreed to hold down the fort for her while she was away. Mike was relatively new to the company and didn't know many people. But he told his friends over beer one night, "All I have to do is see that customer calls get answered, that we address problems that occur with distributors' orders. No sweat. Billi will be back before I know it."

It was near Christmas and the company was introducing three new CD-ROM products, plus a new software package, as well as introducing its first screen-saver product. Per corporate policy, Mike got a form listing the new products, made copies for the staff, then continued to monitor calls and complete reports for senior management about the volume of activity within the department. One day Pete called to find out if anyone had heard from Billi, got Mike on the phone, was told that she was doing well, and hung up. On another occasion, Mac called to check up on Billi, got Mike on the phone, and was told the same. Ditto, Terry. "I know they are old buddies of hers," thought Mike, "but I wish they would leave me alone so I can do her job in her absence."

Of the products being introduced, a problem existed with the screen saver that was only discovered once it was in use. Customers called, were reassured that the company would refund their purchase price if they returned the software, and left Customer Service happy. But meanwhile Terry continued to place ads in computer magazines about the outstanding product line. Mac continued to ship boxes to long-term distributors who had been willing to try out the new product. And Pete's people continued to put the screen saver among the valuable shelf space at dealers. Mike reported the problem but it took three weeks before the information reached Terry, who alerted Pete. Mac was told to hold off further shipments until the problem with the software was corrected.

"No one told me to tell Terry," Mike replied when senior management got wind of the mess and asked for an explanation. And, in truth, that was true. Billi had a wonderful network but she had never encouraged her staff to do the same, or given them an opportunity to work closely with other departments so that the kind of information exchange she had with these department's directors would be had by them with the respective departments' staffers. It never occurred to her that she should not only role-model networking behavior but also verbally advocate it and even give assignments to her staff that would provide communication-building opportunities.

So don't let your network begin and end with you. Find opportunities to have your staff meet with staff of different operations and describe what each group does and identify how each can help the other.

How well do you role-model the behavior you want your employees to practice? To answer that question, put yourself in the shoes of your fellow managers and answer each of these questions about yourself. Do you:

- Listen as well as talk when you chat with your colleagues?
- Introduce yourself to strangers you meet at a corporate or industry meeting, rather than hang back with your pals?
- Break the ice with questions or small talk when surrounded by strangers?
- Visit with colleagues, during which you listen to their concerns and thoughts? Or are such visits made solely in order to ask for something?
- Stay in touch with colleagues from various parts of the organization? Or are colleagues more likely to hear from you only at Christmas or when you need their help?
- Begin phone conversations with, "Am I calling at a good time?"
- Ask your network partner if you can use his or her name in making a further contact, or do you just do it?
- Show a willingness to give help as well as to get it?
- Become a pest, calling over and over again to remind someone of a promised favor?
- Know how to say thank you?

75. Build Bridges to an Outside Network

Incidentally, while we have focused on your internal network, recognize that your network shouldn't end at your corporate door. Actually, the value of your network—and consequently your worth to your colleagues and company—increases when it includes other managers in your field, in your industry, in your town, in your state, in your country, and—in today's global business world—around the world. Whenever you meet with a manager who impresses you, add his or her name to your Rolodex. Scribble some notes on the back of the card about the circumstances in which you met and then file the card by subject matter for future reference.

Outside contacts can be met through such sources as professional organizations, business and management seminars, and trade shows. If you consciously work to develop an open and friendly demeanor, you will increasingly make new contacts and widen your network.

Practice the same kind of bridge building with these individuals as you do with your internal network. At least every quarter, call those people in your outside network to reestablish contact, find out if you can help them—or they can help you—and reaffirm your networking relationship.

While we have focused here on networking for the good of your current organization, we can't leave this chapter without discussing the importance of networking to finding a job elsewhere.

If your internal network is strong, and is well aware of the roadblocks in front of you, you may find its members as helpful in alerting you to opportunities outside your organization as members of your external network. But don't let your colleagues know that you are job hunting. Even the most loyal of friends can't be trusted with that kind of secret.

On the other hand, let members of your external network know about your decision to seek opportunities elsewhere. Indeed, if you have one or two mentors among the network members, seek not only advice in finding a new position but help in determining the kind of position you are best suited for. Suggest lunch with those best positioned to help you. These are the influencers in their own organization. Then broach the topic. Depending on the level of rapport, be direct or subtle. Explain your interest in new challenge, new opportunities. Don't vent about your current position. If a personality conflict between you and your manager is a key factor behind your decision, keep it to yourself. You want to send a positive message through the job community that you have examined the opportunities within your organization, found future challenges lacking, and are looking for new mountains to climb.

For more specific information on getting to the top of that hill, continue to the next chapter.

17

Looking Beyond Today's Job

The purpose of this book is to identify all those skills, abilities, knowledge, traits, and attitudes essential to be a high-value manager in today's leaner organizations. If you already possess all these competencies, then you are ready to look beyond today's position to identify opportunities for advancement and how you can position yourself to be considered for them.

You have three options:

1. You can move out of your existing company to the position you want.
2. You can move up to a position within your organization that either is your ideal job or will lead to it.
3. You can try to create your ideal position by building an entrepreneurial operation within your current organization.

It is easy to get so caught up in the day-to-day office routine that you forget about developmental and career advancement needs, particularly in today's organizations where there are so few chances for job movement. But when opportunities arise—and they will even in the leanest of companies—they will go to those who are best prepared for them. That means not allowing the pressures of the job to distract you from your own professional development and career planning. At the very least, keep on top of the changes in the field. They are occurring so rapidly that it is easy to suffer from professional obsolescence.

Staying abreast of developments in your field, your industry, management, and technological applications is your responsibility, not that of your own manager or organization, no matter how sophisticated your company's training operation is. It is up to you to fight against obsolescence, be adaptable to changes occurring in your organization—including demonstrating a willingness to change your management style so it is in sync with your organization's style—and create a career development plan that provides the competencies you need for today and prepares you for the competencies you will need tomorrow.

As a successful manager, you must:

76. Neutralize obsolescence.

77. Prepare a career plan for promotion within or for a job outside your present organization.

78. Increase your visibility.

79. Seize opportunity when it comes your way.

80. Have a backup plan in the event of dejobbing.

76. Neutralize Obsolescence

While attendance at a seminar or course at a local university may be the first thing you think of as development needs, there are other ways to grow professionally. Do you have young children who demand time at home? Then consider taking a home-study program. Read as much as you can. Start by collecting books and articles relevant to your field and the industry in which your company operates. Don't neglect general management books and articles, either, since they will keep you on top of new management trends and developments, thus helping you to understand developments occurring in your own organization, the reasons for them, and the implications—including career issues—to you. That knowledge can be translated into a more serious action plan for career advancement or development.

If the opportunity arises to attend a formal training program, take it. If you seem open to new knowledge and eager to learn, management is likely to make such opportunities available to you. If you then take the information you have learned and apply it, more such opportunities will come.

Build the skills beyond those you need to do your daily job by involving yourself in a volunteer organization within your community. Besides leadership skills, involvement in civic groups will give you experience in working with people, making presentations, and developing and using the facilitation skills you will need in team structures.

Figure 17-1 is a self-test that allows you to measure your current development efforts. Such assessments should be a continual thing that

Figure 17-1. Career development self-test.

1. Besides this book, how many other management books have you read this year?
2. Have you attended a volunteer training program offered by your company over the last twelve months?
3. Have you volunteered to be a part of a self-managed team in which you can develop your leadership skills, make contacts that may prove valuable in the future, and demonstrate your capabilities?
4. Have you set up a meeting with the staff of a colleague's department or several colleagues' departments to find out more about how each of your operations work?
5. Have you attended an industry conference or joined an association related to your industry? How about attendance at a meeting for individuals in your field? Are you a member of an organization that is related to your field?
6. Have you become involved in some civic or community activity that allows you to meet with managers from other companies? Are you regularly practicing your networking skills outside of your organization?
7. If someone asked senior management who was on top of the new office technology, would you be named?
8. Have you looked for opportunities to perfect your oral and writing skills? Maybe written an article for that trade association's magazine? Offered to speak at an industry conference? Perhaps taken a committee membership position that allows you to influence industry events?

If you haven't done any of these things, include them on your to-do list. Better yet add them somewhere on your personal priority list. Admittedly, self-development requires an investment of personal time, but businesses are constantly changing, and you will need to change just to stay even, let alone be a part of your company's future focus.

Besides maintaining your worth in the job market with a self-development plan, do some research to determine what jobs will be growing, or even be here, five years from now and the implications to your career needs and plans. Where are there new jobs emerging that might interest you? Equally important, which jobs are disappearing? You don't want to build your career plans on the rocky foundation of a job market that is slowly shrinking.

Ask yourself what is most important to you in working. Is it an exciting job where you can be your own boss, even with the risk that might come from failure or unemployment? Or is job security more important if it allows you to use the skills you most enjoy? Is money the be all and end all?

Or, maybe, you have skills that have led to accomplishments outside the office, skills that you enjoy using but to date have not been called on to use in your organization. Is there some career move that would allow you to use these skills to a greater extent?

How about issues like corporate climate or corporate values? Does a tradition-bound institution interest you, or would you be interested in working for a smaller, entrepreneurial firm where you can use your creativity?

helps you to regularly set developmental goals for yourself. Yes, career development and advancement action plans are like any plans you develop on the job; that is, there are goals and subgoals and timed frames to achieve each goal and subgoal.

77. Prepare Your Career Plan

Take a piece of paper and list the results of asking yourself the questions in Figure 17-1: the skills in which you have greatest proficiency, your favorite tasks, the work climate in which you are most comfortable, and the like. Given the realities on that piece of paper, what next job would be most satisfying to you? How likely are you to get such a job now? Over a period of time? Does getting this job entail a move outside your current job? Or will you have to job-hop from one company to another to achieve your objective?

Don't forget your study of career or job patterns. Will the ideal job for you still be there when you are ready for it? If so, then begin to develop an action plan that will gain you that position in the time frame you have identified.

Does that job exist in your current company? If it doesn't, don't forget to include in your plan learning experiences in your current situation that will bring you closer to your goal. If you want to be in charge of product development, for instance, but new product development efforts are few and far between in your organization, until that offer from outside comes look for opportunities to serve on teams whose purpose is to develop new products or services within your own organization. Work your way up to team leader of your own new-product effort. Each success will help make your name more familiar to those who do product development for a living—and closer to your chosen dream job.

If your job goal entails leaving your current position, then your career plan would contain the following information:

- The position you want (your goal)
- Short-term jobs (assignments you might have to take to achieve your goal)
- Action plan
- External network contacts to inform (they can pass the word about your interest in working elsewhere through the industry or field)
- Headhunters to check with
- Rolodex for industry contacts to alert

A career plan for a promotion would take into consideration a key fact: Advancement is the result of a successful mix of three characteristics: competency, visibility, and opportunity. Having the right skills, abilities, knowledge, and attitudes isn't sufficient to get you a new position. You also need to be visible to those who make a promotion decision important to you. And, maybe even more important, you have to be in the right place at the right time (although you may be able to set up circumstances so you create the right place and the right time).

You may also have to make some tough decisions about your personal management style or values if you choose to stay in your current organization. If that company is undergoing changes in both, you will have to make dramatic shifts in your management approach (e.g., from manager to team developer) if you want to stay. You will have to adapt your interpersonal communication and leadership styles to reflect the new organizational design and work process.

78. Increase Your Visibility

Standing Out From the Crowd

Kim's hospital had set up a team to develop an outreach program for the homeless. Kim is one of several head nurses in a substance abuse department. Normally she would not have been chosen to join the team, because her soft-spoken manner and seeming preoccupation with paperwork would make her ill suited for a project calling for strong interpersonal skills. The hospital administrator, Harvey, had planned to choose someone else until he received a written proposal from Kim outlining a press relations campaign to support the outreach program. Kim had been involved in a church venture to shelter the homeless during cold winter months and had discovered she had a knack for getting reporters on the phone and spotting good story angles (to sell the story). She loved it.

When she heard about the task force, Kim thought it was an ideal way to expand her newfound skills and increase her visibility on the job.

As the team came together, Harvey was amazed by Kim's knowledge, skill, creative ideas, problem-solving abilities, and hidden interpersonal skills. The project's success led to creation of an outpatient clinic that took a holistic approach to dealing with the homeless. Kim's involvement led to her being on a more informal work relationship with Harvey. So one morning after a team meeting she felt comfortable telling him she would like to be on the new team that would set up the clinic. Kim became head nurse-coordinator.

Kim's participation with the task force answered a question Harvey never even asked but is often asked in considering managers for promotional opportunities: What can this person do that others can't?

If your goal involves a promotion within your organization, then you need to find ways to demonstrate to those who will make the key decision how your life or job experiences allow you to stand out from the crowd.

Team participation is an excellent way to demonstrate your leadership capabilities, but there are other ways you can. For example, why not consider taking to lunch a colleague who has a problem you know you can help with, and offer that help? Today's companies are looking for problem solvers who will span white space to lend a colleague a hand. So another opportunity might be to identify an orphan task and work independently with another manager, or with a team in addressing that issue. Maybe, too, you might want to set up a continuous improvement team made up of managers from different functions of the organization.

You want to develop a track record of successes that will demonstrate your worth to your organization.

79. Seize Opportunity When You Get the Chance

We've been talking about competency and visibility. But that still leaves the question of opportunity.

Today's leaner organizations don't offer the opportunities for promotion that companies did in the past. Actually, staying where you are is a goal in itself in today's world. So you need to go back to your career plan and determine whether a promotion is realistic right now in your organization.

Maybe it isn't, but what about a lateral move that will put you on a new career path? Could that path eventually lead you to the job goal you identified in your career plan? Or how about even a zigzag path that moves you through the organization?

We tend to think of advancement as only an upward occurrence, but promotion isn't the only way to advance within an organization. Making a lateral move, or several lateral moves over time, makes your capabilities known to senior officers other than your current supervisor, and that can pay off in the long run. A lateral move also gives you firsthand experience in working in different areas of the business, a plus in today's integrated, boundaryless organizations. And, needless to say, if you are plateaued in your current position, a zigzag move bypasses the career roadblocks.

You can also take a more proactive approach to finding opportunities within your organization, creating within the company your own small enclave where you develop a product or offer a service you yourself proposed. Becoming a corporate entrepreneur—or "intrapreneur" as it is called—may seem too unrealistic, but recognize that today's culture rewards risk takers who are willing to pioneer corporate options.

If you seem to be blocked in every direction, unable to move up or sideways, don't forget to expand your opportunities through outside activities. This isn't a wimpish option. Aside from making you feel good and contributing to your community, it gives you access to some high-level networking and expands your skills and accomplishments.

80. Have a Backup Plan

The new core competencies today have to address a reality, which is that you may be out of a job through no fault of your own, no matter how good the skills or the planning. If there is any message that this book should send its readers, it is, "Don't be smug; your job is never safe, no matter what your level, skills, or loyalty to the corporation." Always have a Career Plan B in your survival kit bag, and never stop looking for the next job, even if your boss tells you that your future is secure. The company could get sold, your boss could get fired, and then you are out on your ear.

In such circumstances,

- Increase your networking.
- Call every friend of a friend.
- If no one has a lead for you, ask them if they know of someone who does.
- Don't call for "interviews"; call to do research for job possibilities within targeted industries.
- Use electronic bulletin boards and any other media out there to advertise your availability and talent (even your church and fraternal bulletin boards).

- Identify interim moneymaking projects.
- Always negotiate a dynamite exit package deal (never take the first offer, and have a lawyer look at it).

Your work on your exit package and your negotiating skills set a solid platform on which you can construct your new employment contract with the lucky company that hires you for that better job.

But high-value managers are less likely to be dejobbed than the average manager. Management literature often refers to a company's people as their human assets. Never has that term been more appropriate than when referring to high-value managers—and senior management recognizes it. They are critical to their organization's increasing its market share, sales, and bottom line. High-value managers have the skills, abilities, knowledge, and attitudes that allow them to manage effectively in leaner, restructured organizations during economic downturns and then, in more stable or growth industries, to refocus and help grow their companies. Here we have identified the managerial competencies that companies value. And with cause. And because they will make your management job easier and your career more fruitful, you will recognize their value, too.

Appendix

Core Competency Checklist

Chapter 3

1. Understand any new areas of responsibility and the skills and backgrounds of your new staff members to make the best people and management decisions.
2. Listen actively.
3. Operate on purpose.
4. Emphasize growth and opportunity.
5. Train employees to think critically.

Chapter 4

6. Undertake during the job interview a training needs assessment that is pursued in the event the individual is hired.
7. Structure work groups so they can share their knowledge and skills with one another.
8. Monitor on-the-job learning.
9. Practice action learning.
10. Be willing to take on the role of teacher.

Chapter 5

11. Hold goal-setting sessions.
12. Develop action plans that support the goals of the organization and corporate mission.
13. Prepare contingency plans that ensure that department goals, and therefore corporate objectives, are achieved.
14. Make departmental and corporate goals come alive for staff members by identifying the enablers that will allow the group to contribute to the corporate mission and goals.
15. Maintain enthusiasm for the action plans and objectives.

Chapter 6

16. Deemphasize job title in order to build the kind of cooperative work environment that has proven to be most productive.

17. Effectively use part-time, job-sharing, contracted services, temps, and interns to cope with uneven workflow or tight staff budgets.
18. Offer telecommuting options to full-time staff to increase motivation and/or reduce the need for office space.
19. Lead others in using the new technology.
20. Use the new technology—rather than the tried and true—only where it represents a solid business solution.

Chapter 7

21. Create an environment in which employees are encouraged to use their initiative to remedy problems when they first occur.
22. Undertake problem sensing.
23. View problems as opportunities and mistakes as progress.
24. Practice techniques that enable you to choose the best solution from several good ones.
25. Communicate solutions to the rest of the organization.

Chapter 8

26. Determine customer needs, then develop action plans designed to achieve those needs.
27. Define work quality for staff members.
28. Build individual and team pride in the work to support standards and decisions made about quality.
29. Live the message of quality, both its value and the danger of getting caught up in the chase.

Chapter 9

30. Recognize orphans for what they are.
31. Know how to make judgments about which orphans or problems in white space to devote time to.
32. Draw attention to the orphan or problem without invading another person's turf.
33. Encourage staff members to step into the white space to benefit the department or organization as a whole, and do so yourself.
34. Build synergy by bringing together colleagues to work on the issue. They open communications and begin spanning the white space between job titles or departments.

Chapter 10

35. Know the various stages in which teams operate, their responsibilities in each; and anticipate potential problems prevent them from becoming real ones.

36. Know if a team is truly warranted.
37. Know about the latest technology so you can reduce the need to bring in experts from other organization sites, thus saving work time and travel expenses.
38. Be able to staff a team with the right members and gain their support and cooperation, even when they oversee other departments or functions within the organization.
39. Define the team's mission and its goals and stay on that track through completion of the project.
40. Run meetings smoothly by setting ground rules for communication and behavior within the team structure.
41. Intervene when communication and behavior problems arise.

Chapter 11

42. Tolerate those problems that may be making everyone uncomfortable but are also creating more-productive discussions that might generate a better final team outcome.
43. Differentiate between task-oriented and people-oriented conflicts since your response to each type is different.
44. Steer conflicts away from personalities and toward issues.
45. Be aware of those individuals with the team who are most likely to create conflict and help them to work with you, not against you, for the benefit of the team effort.
46. Understand how proxemics can be applied in team situations to defuse conflicts.
47. Know when a conflict is impeding the team's performance and intervention is called for. Sometimes you can smooth things over during the meeting—but not always.
48. Mediate a conflict between two team members.
49. Meet one-on-one with individual team members who disagree with your leadership or viewpoint to prevent the differences from impeding the team effort.
50. Overcome concerns of members that their ideas won't get a fair hearing when meetings get intense.

Chapter 12

51. Coach for enthusiasm and high performance.
52. Overcome organizational roadblocks to achievement of the team's mission.
53. Oversee training where needed.
54. Use peer pressure to help reform a non–team player or get work associated with the team effort done.

55. Meet and discuss performance problems with members who aren't pulling their weight, even managers who don't report to you directly without alienating them or undermining the rapport among team members.

Chapter 13

56. Be able to present your team and its goals persuasively.
57. Position requests strategically.
58. Negotiate skillfully—get what you want without making enemies.
59. Be flexible—able to adjust your negotiating strategy to achieve results.

Chapter 14

60. Keep the group energized. Most teams begin on an emotional high. You want to maintain that high interest level.
61. Make sure your project contributes to the organization's bottom line.
62. Build positive relationships with other managers.
63. Maintain regular communication with the team's sponsor.
64. Produce compelling reports and presentations that convince senior management of the need to pursue the team's recommendations.

Chapter 15

65. Work smart by thinking through any task before beginning. Responding to a situation without thereby planning can cause you to approach it ineffectively or inefficiently, wasting time and money.
66. Prioritize work to focus on critical tasks.
67. Use subgoals and deadlines to better organize your use of your time.
68. Know how to say no—without alienating those seeking your aid—to request to request for help that will distract from your most important responsibilities. On the other hand know when to say yes and when to say maybe.
69. Know how to avoid the traditional time wasters. Develop good time management habits.
70. Pace yourself so that the stress of today's heavier workloads has a minimal effect on the quality of your life and job performance. Understand your own personal energy peaks and valleys and use that information to most efficiently and effectively complete projects.

Chapter 16

71. Use positive politics to achieve objectives.
72. Cultivate a power base by building your reputation as trustworthy, results-oriented, and fair-minded.
73. Build an internal network.

74. Sustain your network.
75. Build bridges to an outside network.

Chapter 17

76. Neutralize obsolescence.
77. Prepare a career plan for promotion within or for a job outside your present organization.
78. Increase your visibility.
79. Seize opportunity when it comes your way.
80. Have a backup plan in the event of dejobbing.

Index